Contents

Foreword

When I first had children I wish there had been some kind of reference book for me as a father. I would have loved to find a book that offered me tips or advice on how I could be a good father to my children. I didn't have a role model to copy, as my father was very often away from home, and I only saw him on very rare occasions during my childhood. Sometimes, this could be as little as once a month. I missed that interaction at the time, but I didn't really realise what I was missing.

I have been inspired by the quality of life that a deep relationship with one's own children can give a father, and wanted to share this experience with other fathers. I attribute this to my three children and the sense of pure fulfilment and happiness they have given me over the years, and continue to give me every day. At first glance the father and child relationship appears very simple, but actually, it is extremely complex. It underpins the strongest emotional bond anyone ever forms in their life, namely that between a parent and a child.

This book is not written with any verifiable scientific research as its foundation, but is based purely on my life experience with my three children. My inspiration was to be able to write a practical father and child guide, offering help, tips and advice on this complex and vital relationship. To offer advice on how to maximise the quality of the relationship between children and their fathers. If it can help improve the quality of relationship between just one child and his father, then I will have achieved my goal.

The relationship between parents and their children within the family unit underpins the whole fabric of society. So many ills in society can be directly linked to problems within the family unit. Very often, this will be because of an absentee father in the household. If the relationship is strong and stable, it will have a positive effect for many years into the future. A close and loving dynamic will benefit you, your child and society in general. If you are to get the most out of being a father, you have to be prepared to take on every aspect of the job; however challenging it is, and be involved 100% in every area of your child's life. If you do this and are totally committed to being the best dad possible to your children, it will be the most rewarding thing that you will ever have experienced.

During my own childhood, my father travelled a lot, so he missed virtually all the key moments throughout my younger years. As a youngster, I always felt our relationship was lacking something, because he wasn't there very often. The strong communication and understanding between us was lacking, because his work took him away from home so often. This was carried right the way through to when he died. Although in later years I saw more of him, the truly close bond was not there. There was always something missing. He was unable to share those key defining moments with me as I grew up, and I really missed the interaction of sharing my special achievements and intimate moments with him. The ones that only a father can share with his child.

I therefore decided that when I wanted to have children I would be as involved as possible in every aspect of their lives. I was determined not to make the same mistakes as my father, with my own children. Whatever that involved, I would be there 'in the thick of it', make whatever sacrifices needed to be done, and share all those special moments that my father had missed out on with me. Despite all these good intentions, I was terrified when my first child was born. I thought I was ready and had done as much as I felt I could do to prepare, but nothing can really get you ready for the arrival of a new-born baby.

Whether this meant changing that first nappy, putting it on wrongly and having no idea what I was doing; which was what happened. It was a real disaster with everyone getting very messy and wet. Or playing in the dad's football match; actually I even played in a mother's netball match without knowing a single rule of netball! It was a real eye opener. Or staying up till 2.00 am in a dark open field in the middle of nowhere, holding a camera tripod steady. All because my son needed some crystal clear photographs of the moon for his 'A' level course……. No matter what, I was determined to be there.

I have suggested helpful tips, advice and ideas on how to cope with certain everyday situations or circumstances which arise. These have worked for me and enhanced the quality of the relationship that I have enjoyed with my children. In this book you will learn about many anecdotes and discover practical tips which have helped me avoid degenerating situations from developing. These have saved both my children and I on many occasions from being overtaken by anger, frustration and despair.

One of the most important things you will need as you bring your child up is the word "Sorry". Use it wisely and sincerely and it will help you recover a potentially disastrous situation from developing and from getting completely out of hand. Never be so 'pig headed' as to refuse to say sorry to your children, it really works……. but you must mean it.

There will be parts of this book where you say to yourself "I know that". Then there will be other parts where you say "that's a good idea, I will try that". I am sure that you are doing many things to be the best father possible to your children, or you wouldn't be reading this book now. However, I wish I had been able to find a reference book like this when my own children were born.

A book which offered me anecdotes, tips and strategies to use, to help me manage the day to day situations that occurred with my children. I am sure you know that there are challenges everyday as a father, and the dynamic of the relationship evolves and develops as every day passes. If a book like this had existed when I started my journey as a father, I could have saved myself a lot of trouble, mistakes and heartache, and I have certainly made my fair share of them.

Of course, you will say 'making mistakes as you go along is how you learn', and this is very true. However, with your children, mistakes can be very costly in terms of long term damage if you get it wrong. A throw away comment about body shape or attitude at the end of a heated discussion may lead to a complex which can develop over many years, and be carried into adulthood.

So, if there are strategies to avoid this, then it has to be worth knowing about them. Having said this, I made many mistakes along my journey in fatherhood, but I learnt from them and have tried to make sure I didn't make them again. There are many anecdotes in this book which demonstrate this, but I still make some mistakes, as my journey as a father isn't finished. But I am continuing to learn as I go on.

I don't claim to know everything about being a good father, but what I do know is that a strong father-child relationship is both vital and incredibly rewarding. When I look back on the childhood and development of my three children (they are all adults now) I see that the relationship we enjoy still remains extremely close. We have very open communication together and have gone through all the various stages of development together. Of course, there were the inevitable ups and downs that a child goes through as it grows up, and you will read about many of them in the following chapters.

I have always felt I was learning as much from them as they were learning from me. Today, that dynamism still brings a huge smile to my face when I think about the things they have taught me over the years. So I write this book, to a degree, in a selfish manner, really. It is what I would have liked to have had available to me when I first decided to have children.

Therefore, I dedicate this book to my wife and three children. Also, to all those people who decide to have children and struggle; working really hard to try and bring their families up in the best possible way.

The aim of this book is to give an objective look at being a father in a relatively

light-hearted manner. This is because fatherhood must always be about having fun with your children. It's not about being too serious, although of course you can never treat fatherhood as something trivial. There are always serious issues to be addressed and considered as a father and you can never forget this. However, remember a smile and a laugh can help you overcome almost all of the challenging situations that will present themselves to you as your child grows up.

Hopefully, you will want to keep this book near you wherever you and your children go. Then you will have on-hand an instant help or possible solution for whatever day to day situation presents itself to you. Where you feel you need a little inspiration in relation to your children, this book can offer you help or an idea on how to handle it.

As the title of this book suggests, there are everyday situations which present themselves to you as a dad and for which you sometimes need a potential new solution. Many people see becoming a dad as being 'thrown in at the deep end', and this book will hopefully 'help you swim'. Hopefully, you only need to use these measures when the situation really requires them. I have referred to the following three categories regularly throughout the Chapters, and these are:

Firstly, **'Life Jacket'** – this is worn every day, like an Insurance policy or good daily habits.

Secondly, **'Lifebuoy'** – this is thrown in at the right moment, when you are struggling, and will allow you to 'keep your head above water long enough for you to get back to dry land'.

Thirdly, **'Life Raft'** – this is for major incidents, and could save your life. It is used when you are experiencing very difficult times and need emergency help.

So this book starts at a very early age, and actually before your first child is born. The moment a child is conceived, your role as a father starts. How you react to your partner when you learn she is pregnant can determine how involved you will be as a father. If you unreservedly share the joy and support her fully during pregnancy, you will have started off well and will already be getting prepared for being a father.

Chapter 1

<u>**Help - The Nuts and Bolts of Fatherhood**</u>

In the past, fathers didn't show their emotions like mothers did. Boys had to follow in their footsteps, and show the 'British Stiff Upper Lip'. Girls were considered different from boys and allowed to be emotional. Yet life is full of emotion no matter what sex you are. Whether it is happiness or sadness, elation or despair, you should never be afraid to show your emotions as a father. Children need to know that their father experiences the same type of emotions that they do. They also need to be able to see you showing those emotions.

Doing this prevents any subconscious mental barriers being constructed within the vital relationship between you as a father, and your child. Be very tactile with your children, they need physical contact with you as their father just as much as they do with their mother.

Don't be afraid to give your child a hug when you see her, or to always kiss her goodnight when she goes to bed, irrespective of what age she is, 2 or 22. For a child, at the beginning, it is totally normal that this should happen. After all, you are her father. You are one of the two most important people in her life and you should remain as that until she starts her own life with her own partner and has children of her own. Even then, that bond will never be lost if you have created a relationship built on substance, respect and love.

Life Jacket

By showing your feelings and being proud of them, it stops any emotional distance growing between you.

How often do you hear children say to their parents "you never listen to me?" If you really want to, it's easy to always listen carefully to what your child is saying. This philosophy is your chance to make sure your children know from a very early age that you do listen to them. They need to know that their contribution to the family dynamic is just as important as yours. It is always a two-way relationship and you must never forget that.

Answer your child's questions

If your child asks a question, it is because he wants to know the answer. Of course, depending on the age of your child you respond appropriately, but never brush off their question as not being important. The fact that your child asks you a question shows that he is curious. He has a desire to discover the world he is growing up in and a need to interact with you, and you with him. The question is important to your child based upon his current points of reference, or he would not have asked it.

He will value your undivided attention so much, which will become evident in later years when you ask him a question, or need an answer. He will give it to you, because that has always been the way you have treated him. As his father, you lead by example.

It is at a very early age that you should set the ground rules for the quality of communication between you and your children. This will determine what happens throughout their whole childhood. If you get this right at the start of their lives it will reap immeasurable benefits for the quality of your relationship together in later years. This will be very evident during their teenage years, when the challenges are very different, and can sometimes seem insurmountable for both of you.

Lifebuoy

So stop what you are doing, however inconvenient it is (as long as it is safe to do so), and give your child your undivided attention. Answer him honestly, although you should take his age into consideration, but you must always answer his question.

Think of the amount of times you have heard other fathers say to their child "ask me later", or "go and ask your mother". By doing this, you are sending a subliminal message to your child. 'I do not have time for you right now', or 'I'm not interested in what you want to know', or even 'it doesn't concern me'. Potentially, this can be the start of the construction of subconscious barriers to communication with your child, which as he gets older, will be very hard to overcome.

Your child will forgive you

This is a major mistake and one that I made when my first child was about 5 years old. He asked me "how does the engine of a car work?" I had just come in from work, and was very tired, so I told him to "ask me later". He became very upset and interpreted it as I didn't care and wasn't interested in his question. It took me many months of talking to him, explaining that I was wrong not to answer him, before he finally forgave me. That situation was totally avoidable.

The whole dynamic of society is underpinned by the relationship we as parents have with our children as they grow up. Everything your child does concerns you and therefore you should be interested in every little aspect of their lives. How often have you heard people say "it is the details that make the difference?" Giving your child the attention and time she needs is a big detail. This will make a huge difference in how successful and meaningful your relationship with her is for the rest of her life.

Negativity can be a downward spiral and brings other people down with you, so always try to be positive with your children; even though it can be very difficult. In fact, it is almost impossible when they are being naughty. But try to turn a negative situation into a positive one where you can both learn from it and draw some real pluses. Offer your children incentives for good behaviour, not always a punishment for bad behaviour. Of course, if they are badly behaved you need to punish them. However, you need to make them understand that there are boundaries which must not be crossed. They need to know that there are consequences to the decisions that they make, but always make sure it is proportional to the misdemeanour.

Your child needs to understand what is acceptable behaviour and what is not. This is very important as she grows up. But you need to be consistent as well. If it is unacceptable today, it is also unacceptable tomorrow.

An example of a positive incentive that I used which always worked was "if you keep your room tidy every week this month, we will go to the children's farm at the end of it", (when they are 3 to 7 years old). When they are a bit older, it could be to "go to the cinema to see the latest Blockbuster" (8 - 15 years old)".

<u>Train Spotting</u>

My eldest son used to love to go and watch the trains and count the carriages when he was a toddler, like lots of young children. This simple pleasure costs nothing but your time but will be really enjoyed by your child. I used to say to him that if he ate all his vegetables up at supper this week, we would go and watch the trains at the weekend. He loved this incentive, and always ate all his food. He still eats everything today and will always try any new dish at least once. Although he loved the trains when he was small, now he's working, he's not so keen on rush hour ones. By reinforcing positive and good behaviour when your child is very young, this philosophy will stay with him throughout his entire life.

Divide and Conquer

If you make the mistake of contradicting your partner in front of your children, this will have negative repercussions for your relationship with your children for many years to come. Always work together as a team with the mother of your children, as children will consistently try to exploit differences of opinion between their parents. The expression 'Divide and Conquer' applies very much to the relationship your children have with you and their mother. Not unlike many aspects of life generally, your goal will be easier to achieve if you can split the opposition.

This will become particularly important when they become teenagers, when the challenges become more serious. If you fail to do this when they are very young it will make the task of maintaining discipline that much harder when they get older. Remember, it is not a contest between you and your partner to be the most popular with your children. You are a team bringing up children and it is vital that you behave like one.

It is your duty to be the best possible father to your children and to complement their mother. Your role is very different to hers, but is equally as important, so teamwork is key. It is like a football match. If everyone on the team knows what they have to do and plays and supports each other, they have a much better chance of winning. The sum of your individual parts as a father and a mother is greater if you work together, than if you work alone. It takes two parents working closely together to bring up children, which is why it is so important for you to be fully involved right from the start.

Your child will observe and copy everything you do, all the time. Boys particularly, will observe very closely what their father is doing. Remember you are his idol, particularly when he is very young, so absolutely everything you do matters to him. Your child's behaviour will reflect the way you are and how you behave on a day to day basis.

Life Jacket

If you are always shouting, this will be considered normal behaviour, or if you can't be bothered about things, your children will simply copy you. So you need to be a strong, positive and good role model for them. "Your children are what you make them". You must never forget this. It is key to your role as their father. Here is a list, not an exhaustive one by any means, of a few tips to ensure you are a good role model for them.

Being a Role Model for your Children

Work hard at what you do (paid or unpaid).

Be nice to people, even if they irritate you.

Be polite and kind to everyone you meet.

Be tolerant of other people's differences with you.

Always help others if you are able to.

Never be aggressive, nasty or react violently.

Be a good citizen and respect the laws of the country.

Be a good listener and give your time to people you meet.

If you haven't got anything nice to say about someone, then don't say it at all.

Chapter 2

Help - I'm going to be a Dad!

Although not always obvious, the relationship between a father and a child begins before your child is born. We know that babies can hear what is going on outside their mother's tummy, so it is important to talk to your child before it is born. Interact with your unborn child and feel it move inside its mother's tummy. This is something very intimate and special, as it allows you to start bonding with your baby before she is born. You will feel that you are an integral part of the development of your child's new life before she actually arrives into this world. Your partner will also love this.

Talking to your partner's tummy

Hearing your voice as well as its mother's is part of the bonding process. Your unborn child hears its mother's voice every time she says anything while it is developing inside her, but it is also important that your child hears your voice as often as possible as well. Your baby also needs to feel your touch as you caress it through its mother's tummy. The amazing journey of fatherhood begins now.

It takes two to make a baby and it definitely takes two to bring one up. The easy part is making it, the hardest, and also the most rewarding part, is bringing it up. Getting to the end of the road, if there ever really is an end of the road, is an incredible achievement and a truly satisfying experience.

So I would strongly recommend that when it's time for your baby to be born, that you do your utmost to be present at the birth, if at all possible. The three most moving and profound moments of my life were the births of my own children and I am sure it will be the same for you. I can remember each one as if they occurred just yesterday. I know very occasionally circumstances can be out of your control and therefore it isn't possible, but with good planning, you can try to minimise the chance of you missing it.

Life Jacket

If you possibly can, make sure you are present at the birth of your baby. It will be the most profound experience of your life.

If you can do this you will feel you are an integral part of the arrival of your children into this world, and that you aren't a peripheral figure to everything going on. Try to hold your baby before the umbilical cord is cut. She will see your face before she sees her mothers. Of course, it is not a competition to see who is loved the most, but it is important that the bonding between you and your child is cemented the moment she comes into this world.

The miracle of human life

This is not to mention the sheer magic and awe at being present at such an intimate moment in the miracle of human life. It will be the most meaningful and emotionally charged event in your entire life and the memory of your child's arrival into this world will remain with you for the rest of your life. The significance of such a moment can never be underplayed for you as a father, and yet it will seem to go by in the blink of an eye.

Before the birth you may have lots of qualms about seeing blood, or seeing your partner in pain and being there in such a highly charged emotional situation, so you may be hesitant initially. The significance of the occasion once your partner goes into labour will make you forget about all those concerns. The more you realise that this is something so life changing, and so profound, the more you will want to be there. It will be even more meaningful for you, as you have been communicating with your baby and touching him through his mother's tummy for the last six months.

To be there at the birth of your child will be an amazing experience for you. In fact, it will be one of the most moving experiences that you will ever have been witness to at any time in your life. So I would strongly recommend that you, as a father to be, make sure that you are there at the birth of your child and witness his arrival into this world.

Hold him as soon as he is born and you will see and feel immediately the intimate and unique bond between you. When you first look into his eyes as his father and reflect that this little being is part of you, it will start immediately. You will never ever forget that moment. It will remain as vivid in your mind for many years into the future, as the day he was born.

Life Jacket

Try to hold your baby before the umbilical cord is cut.

The whole crux of my book and the message I really want to communicate to you as a father, is that if you want to enjoy and get the most out of being a dad for both you and your children, then get totally involved with them. Do this right from the beginning and find ways, however small, of being part of every aspect of your child's life.

Traditionally, in the family, the father has worked away from home during the day and the mother has looked after the baby. Today, even though that has changed significantly, you should always make a big effort to be active and present every day in your child's life, as well as all through the key development stages in her life. This is key, whatever your life circumstances are.

The Bonding Process pre-Birth

Always give your child time, whatever you're doing. Interact with her, stop and listen to her and start this before she is born. Talk to your unborn child every day while she is still in the womb. Remember, your baby can hear you, so she will be getting used to your voice for when she first sees you.

Stroke your child through her mother's tummy every day. Let her feel the movement and touch of your hand through your partner's skin. Don't be afraid to feel her little feet or hands, and to gently poke her, so she can really sense you. Occasionally, she will have hiccups, and as she grows and the birth date gets nearer you may be able to see the whole of your partner's tummy move.

You can talk to her at the same time as you do this. Your partner will also love this intimacy and interaction between you and your child. She will really feel that she is going through pregnancy with you and not doing it all on her own. Start listening to your baby by putting your ear to her mother's tummy. This is a good discipline for later on in life, when your listening skills will be very much needed.

Make sure you have the Birth Plan with you

Discuss with your partner how involved you will be with your baby once it is born. Reassure her that she will have your full support, and that you are in this together. Do this as often as possible, as sometimes during pregnancy she will feel as if she is doing it all on her own. She will never get tired of hearing you say this.

Prepare a full Birth Plan well in advance of the due date of your baby.

Discuss all the options for pain relief and type of delivery that your partner wants. Also make sure that you agree in advance that whatever happens, apart from an emergency situation (whereby it is the Doctors who will decide), that it is you who will ensure that the Plan is adhered to. This is despite what your partner may say or do during the childbirth procedure. It is very important to agree this beforehand, as giving birth is so emotionally charged; not to mention painful for your partner, that she, and possibly you, won't always make rational decisions in the heat of the moment.

Also, you need to prepare fully for the arrival of your child from a practical perspective. This can mean ensuring you have things like a carrier seat, a pram, baby-grows, milk sterilising equipment, or a cot, ready for the arrival; not to mention diapers and creams. This is not an exhaustive list, but gives you an idea as a starting point. Your partner will expect you to have all of this under control while she concentrates on the hard part of giving birth.

You also need to prepare for the arrival of your baby on an emotional level. When your baby arrives it will change the immediate nature of your relationship with your partner, or at least for the first few months while the dust settles. You will need to do a lot of listening to your partner as the birth nears, helping her cope psychologically as well as physically. Be totally supportive and be extremely tolerant. Remember, it is not easy to give birth to a baby. Say nice little things to her, pay her compliments, tell her she looks beautiful, it will really make her feel good, as inside she will be very nervous and feeling that you really care will help enormously.

Actually, the arrival of your child will probably change the dynamic of your relationship with your partner for good. It will never be quite the same again. In fact, it will be even more enriching and enjoyable once you get used to having another little person around, getting involved in your life together. Initially, it will seem like your intimate relationship has disappeared for good, so make sure you enjoy your time together before your baby is born.

I have often heard it said "if men had to give birth then there would be no brothers or sisters on this earth". You will witness why this is true during the birth of your baby, so make sure you remember it. As a father, I can tell you having witnessed the birth of my three children, I would not want to give birth to one, let alone three. I still marvel today at how my wife gave birth three times to bring our children into this world.

Chapter 3

Help - My Baby Has Arrived

Congratulations, you're a father. Let's have a look at those vital early and later months before your baby gets mobile and becomes a Toddler. These are some of the most important times in your role of being a great dad.

In fact, the first year and a half are so vital that if you muck them up, it could have a negative impact on the next 18 years for both you and your child. In this chapter I will share with you seven areas of 'must do's' from when your child is born and you take him home.

Arriving Home

As soon as your baby arrives, get totally involved and be there for your partner. While your child is a baby it is very important for you to play with him, bath him, change his nappies, and share those key moments with him.

Getting Happy with the Nappy

You may be thinking 'me, changing a nappy? Can that really be a key moment with my baby?' Yes, it really can.

You'll get to experience some very intimate, funny and messy times, but they'll also be times that you'll recount and laugh about for the next twenty years. They may not all be 'rosy' moments, and nothing can prepare you for your first really smelly one. In fact, you'll wonder how something so small and cute can produce something so revolting and toxic. The temptation may be to let your partner take care of the nappy changes.

Life Jacket

Your partner does most of the input so do your share of the output.

Remember to make sure that the place where you change your baby presents no risk of him wriggling off, falling and hurting himself.

I made the mistake once of wanting to change my son's nappy just before I had to rush off and catch a train for an important meeting in London. I was fully suited, with a crisp clean shirt and wearing one of my favourite ties. The nappy was off and he was lying there smiling and I was doing my best to entertain him when suddenly, with no warning at all, a jet of warm yellow liquid shot up all over my suit, shirt and tie. My first reaction was fury and I shouted to my wife to come and finish the job.

I gave my son 'that look'. But no matter how upset I was, he was still smiling at me and as I looked at him my anger subsided immediately. I still changed the nappy (and all my clothes), missed my train, was late for my meeting, but laughed about it all day. There are worse things that can happen to you.

It's not worth getting upset or annoyed if your child spills milk on you either. Or worse still, vomits on your work clothes after a feed. It happened to me many times, but it was all worthwhile to see his little smile as he got rid of the wind in his tummy.

Lifebuoy

Always make sure you ask your partner if she has just fed your baby before you arrive and did she manage to wind him afterwards?

In my excitement to see my children after a day at work I almost always forgot to ask whether he had been winded after his feed. In my enthusiasm for a cuddle it has caused many accidents.

One Friday evening I came home after a day at work and picked up our daughter. As usual, I didn't ask any questions, put her on my shoulder, where she promptly vomited all down the back of my jacket. It was Friday, so I was pretty relaxed and just changed my jacket. My wife and I were going to neighbours for drinks, the babysitter had arrived and with a new jacket on, off we went.

After 45 minutes of hugs and hellos we were chatting to a group of friends when suddenly one said, "Mark, what the heck's that on your trousers?" You guessed it! My little princess had puked right down my trouser legs too, and I hadn't noticed. At that moment everyone worked out what the unusual smell had been (I think the parents of babies become immune to the scent of milky vomit) and a bit of ribbing and exaggerated gagging ensued.

Babies will be sick on you. Of course, this may mean you have to take your stuff to the dry cleaners, but who cares. Your child didn't do it on purpose, even if she is smiling at you and has that unspoken look on her face 'caught you out there dad didn't I?' She certainly didn't have any ulterior motives for doing it, so don't blow it out of perspective.

The year or so before they start walking and become Toddlers is probably the most physically tiring time for you as parents. They are so dependent on you both and they need you in order to exist and survive. So expect them to be very demanding.
In the first few months after your child is born it is especially challenging for his mother. She has to breastfeed him, change him regularly when you are not around and she may possibly have some post-natal depression to cope with.

This is your opportunity to really take charge of the situation, relieve your partner and jump into the role of being a Father in its entirety. It allows you to show to your child and your partner that you are just as important to him as his mother. He will be learning while you do this, that you can be relied upon to be there as well. It will also reassure your partner that you are in this together and that she can rely on you to take the pressure off her.

It can be very tiring to care for your child during the first year or so, particularly if they suffer from colic at night after they go to bed. Some babies suffer terribly from wind and for the first 18 months might wake you up 5 or 6 times every night. This is when you should share night duty so you can both survive.

Happy Birth Day

Your child's Birthday is so momentous, it may even pass you by in a total daze as you come to terms with what has just happened. Remember, this isn't only the most important day in your child's life, but also for you. Nothing can prepare you for the whirlwind which has just entered your life. Your baby may be very small, but you can be sure he will demand the most attention of everyone in your household for many years. Here's some simple ideas that will help you to manage with your child during the first year or so.

Where's my seat for the emotional rollercoaster?

If at all possible, try to be there at the birth, it will allow you to bond instantly with your child and equally as important, your partner will know she is not alone. Take charge of the situation, and be fully involved. Listen to what the midwife is telling you to do and make sure that your partner knows you are there supporting her.

Try to stick to the Birth Plan (See chapter 2) as much as possible, despite what your partner may say once she has gone into labour. Remember, she made the plan with you and decided in a rational manner how she wanted the whole birth process to go. Be sensitive, but be strong. Of course, if there is a medical emergency then the medical staff will tell you what needs to be done. But if not, stick with what was planned.

Be ready to see a side of your partner that you may never have seen before. And believe me, I was stunned by what I witnessed. My wife was (and still is today) very calm, and never uses colourful language. But during the birth I heard her say things and use words that I didn't even know were in her vocabulary. It was a really steep learning curve for me and was quite unnerving at the time. But if you are worried by what you hear or see, just ask the midwife and she will reassure you that this is normal behaviour. Whatever your partner says, screams or shouts, your midwife has heard worse.

My friend Michael Heppell recounted to me once, that when his wife was giving birth, he kept tapping the side of the bed much to the annoyance of his wife. At one point he meant to ask how she was getting on. But it came out as "Can you get a move on?" Needless to say Mrs Heppell could have happily killed him at that point.

Keep Calm and Carry On

The pain of childbirth is so intense that in that moment your partner will say and want to do things that you have never seen or heard her do before. Reason goes completely out the window. Your job is to reassure her all the time, ignoring what she is saying and stay calm at all times. Her behaviour will also depend on what type of pain killers she has opted for in the Birth Plan. In any case, staying calm at all times will help everyone in the room stay less stressed.

the umbilical cord is cut, try to be the one to place her in your partner's arms. This will reinforce the sense of bonding between you all and that you are all in it together.

As soon as you are left alone with your partner and new baby, spend some time telling her how well she has done throughout the childbirth. She will be feeling absolutely exhausted, elated and yet maybe a bit melancholic. By supporting, encouraging and talking to her, and being really positive, you will reassure her just how well she has done and make her feel good about the whole experience; even if she has no energy left. You will also feel exhausted and elated, as you will have been riding the proverbial 'emotional rollercoaster' too.

Time to go Home

When you arrive home with your baby for the first time, if you have animals (dogs specifically), immediately bring your baby to be introduced to the family pet.

This will make your dog feel fully included in the arrival of the new family member and help to prevent any jealousy occurring. If you don't push it away, it will create its own bond for looking after and protecting your child. Your baby will also immediately and subconsciously start to learn not to feel threatened by dogs. In later life, this will be a good social skill as she will be more comfortable around animals.

When we had our first baby and brought him home from the hospital, we placed him in his carrier seat on the floor in the middle of the lounge. We then called our dog over to see him. She sniffed him and looked at him, and sniffed him again, and understood that he was a new addition to the family, and was no threat to her.

From that day onwards until she died 10 years later, she slept under his cot initially and then his bed, and 'protected' him. She would rotate rooms virtually every night once we had all three of our children.

Of course, this might not be possible in some households depending on the breed of dog. Also, if your pet is an outdoor one it will be slightly different. However, when you do go outside with your baby for the first time make sure that you introduce your new arrival to the family pet. It worked very well for us.

Prior to your baby's arrival, talk to your older children about having a new member of the family. It is very important to include them in all the attention their new sibling is getting. It will make them feel good towards their new sister and be really positive about her arrival.

For years after our daughter was born our oldest son always remembered the Thomas the Tank Engine train set 'his new sister bought him'. He loved her for that, (Toddlers can be so fickle) and never got jealous when we were giving her attention, because he understood she was smaller than him and 'needed to be looked after'.

Split shifts will help you sleep better

Get your partner to express breastmilk before you both go to bed. This will mean that you can give her a break at night, and feed your baby from the bottle. The fact that you will be feeding your baby will also allow you to bond closer with him.

I read a fascinating piece of research from Unicef which underlined the fact that feeding a new born child either from the breast or the bottle with expressed breast milk, is integral to the bonding process between a baby and his parents. It is also very important to share this load, as you need to prevent your child's mother getting too tired. If she does, she may not be able to produce sufficient quantity and quality of breast milk to satisfy your child's hunger. He will then end up becoming frustrated, agitated and still hungry. This will then become even more tiring on you both as he will cry for more food and will not settle. It will become a vicious circle.

Split Shifts may only be needed for a few months, as your baby could well sleep through the night from just a few weeks. If not, it may not be until your child starts to eat solid food. If you plan it well, it is possible to manage such short nights, so don't worry.

When it is your baby's bed time, stay with him for a few minutes, and sing him nursery rhymes. He will love to hear 'Daddy's' voice as well as 'Mummy's' before he goes to sleep. He will listen to and appreciate your dulcet tones as if you are the greatest Diva that ever sang. Your voice really will be 'music to his ears', so don't be shy. Remember, you are just as important to him as his mother is.

You will be amazed at just how quickly you recall the lyrics of the songs you sang in your childhood if you do this regularly. In fact, this can be quite soothing for you as well. This is very high quality time that you are spending together at the end of the day and part of the start of a vital, intense and incredibly rewarding relationship that you as a Father will have with your child.

World class warbling doesn't always work

Sometimes you will find that your baby is not settling very quickly; yes, even after your world class warbling. Usually he will have fallen asleep by the time you finish singing, or at least be very calm, but sometimes he just won't settle. It used to worry me a lot until my friend Peter said to me "Don't be afraid to leave your baby crying in his cot for a few minutes. He will be fine".

I felt better hearing him tell me that. Peter had older children and they were still alive. It is really tempting to keep checking every minute, but this will only make matters worse. Very often he will settle on his own as he gets used to his environment.

If he really is in distress, it will continue for longer than 10 minutes, even though it still might just be a little trapped wind. You will get to know whether it is more than just colic the more experienced you become with handling your child. But if you are starting to get worried, pick up the phone. Never be afraid to ring your parents, in-laws or friends who have older children than yours. Just hearing that it's ok, normal and not to worry, can be very re-assuring.

Of course, you and your partner know your baby best. If after 10 minutes or so he is still crying, pick him up. This will normally have an instant calming effect, and after a few minutes you should be able to put him back in his cot. You may need to sing him a few songs again, but he won't mind hearing the same ones.

A battle of wits

Sometimes your baby will actually be testing you just to see what will happen. This subconscious behaviour will happen on many occasions and how you react will affect how he will behave at bedtime in the future. Remember, during these first few months everything is a learning curve for you and your baby. So how you react will determine what happens in the future. It's often a battle of wits and one that you have to win.

What should I do if my Baby is under the weather?

If your baby has a temperature and is a little under the weather don't make the mistake of wrapping him up. It will make him even hotter and make matters worse. It seems crazy now, but we did that with our oldest child and couldn't understand why his temperature was getting worse. The first time this happened it was very stressful for us as we just couldn't reduce his temperature. Eventually, we called the hospital and got some very sound advice which worked. We put it into practice immediately. Every time any of our children ever got a temperature from then onwards we just followed this simple advice.

If the temperature proves difficult to reduce, you can use a moist cloth to dab his forehead, neck and body, and this will help bring it down. You can even use a fan as a cool breeze will also work to reduce it. If all these measures fail then you should of course seek medical assistance.

Having Fun with your Baby

Don't be afraid to change your baby's nappies right from the very first time she arrives home. Make it a fun time as well, by singing little songs, or tickling your baby's feet or tummy while you do it. Subconscious bonding occurs while you do this, as she smiles at you, and you smile back at her. Each time you do this you are reinforcing the link and love between you. Such a mundane yet intimate task as changing a nappy lays the seeds for a very strong and involved relationship between you and your child as she grows up.

Whenever possible, try to be present for every bath time. Get used to holding your baby in the water while you wash him. This will give you the confidence to handle him in a potentially dangerous situation and create trust between you and your baby. It will be another reinforcement for your growing bond together as well.

Make bath time fun. This is a part of the day that you and your baby can really enjoy. Once the job of being washed is out the way, play time can begin, even when your baby is very small. Have little floating ducks or balls that he can push around the bath while you, at all times, hold him very firmly.

Lifebuoy

Let him splash you while you pretend to be shocked. Your baby will love the staged expressions on your face as you get wet.

Take charge of your Baby

While your baby sleeps during the day you can take charge once more and encourage your partner to have a rest or sleep at the same time. If it is at the weekend you should also try to have a rest during the day. Your partner shouldn't worry about household chores; they can be done later when you are both around and have a bit of energy. It is very important that you and your partner can recharge your batteries when you are able to, as your child will be very demanding when he is awake.

Don't overdo the 'Goo Goo Ga Ga'

Of course, there is nothing wrong with making soft cooing noises to your baby, which he will find very soothing, but you should also speak real words to him. When your baby is awake, talk to him like you would talk normally to any small child. Remember he is learning from you all the time you are with him. Your child's brain is like a sponge and he is soaking up everything you do and say to him.

If your child is agitated and won't settle during the day, lie her along the top of your forearm. Place her with her head next to the outside of your elbow, with you holding the top part of her leg firmly. Not too firmly though, to avoid cutting off the blood circulation. This will allow you to move around the house and continue to do the things that need to be done. The movement of being on your arm and moving with you around the house will also be very soothing for your baby. She will love this and will settle even though you are moving around. She may even fall asleep with the warmth of your arm next to her.

Your baby is learning from you all the time and needs to know that her father is good fun to be with as well as her mum. She will love playing with you, so don't be afraid to do this with her, even though she is very small. Acquire a 'play mat' and 'clip on gym' (new or second-hand) and use this as a means to play, learn and have fun with each other. This is also very therapeutic and will relax you both, so you really enjoy the quality time together.

Lifebuoy

The key thing to do here is to lie on your back beneath it, with your baby lying on your chest or stomach, or even next to you, if it is too low. You can then both look up at the toys on the bar above you, and play with them together.

In your living area, if you can find some space, try to create a play pen for your child; about 6 square metres in size. You can buy these new or second-hand. Get one which has some little toys attached to the inside of the barriers. Make sure you have some padding on the floor however, for when he topples over, which he inevitably will. This will create a safe area that you can feel confident about leaving your child in while you and your partner get some well-deserved 'down time'.

You'll need this relaxation time to remain sane. It gets your child used to playing alone and not getting bored too quickly. It will also stop him demanding attention from you all the time. You shouldn't feel guilty about leaving him on his own for a while, as he needs to learn that mummy and daddy are not constantly at his disposal. By doing this it will then allow you and your partner to concentrate on yourselves for a little.

When you get back from work, always take a few moments to greet your baby and spend some time with her. It will give her mother some well-earned rest after another tiring day. When you do get home, or come into the house after being away, don't just flop down into a chair and say "I'm tired, I need a rest", even if it is true. Make that little effort to hug and kiss your baby, say "hello" as only a father can, and encourage your partner to have a rest for a few minutes.

By taking the load off your partner immediately once you get home, you will free her up to spend a little time on herself, where she can chill out and be totally selfish. All parents need to be able to do this from time to time. She will start to relax, unwind and feel good about herself. It's vital to encourage your partner to spend time on herself especially if once your baby has gone to bed you want her to spend time on you.

This will definitely help improve your sex life when you go to bed, as it will seem like sex has been put on hold since your baby arrived in the family. Your partner will know when she is ready to start having an intimate relationship with you again and a lot will depend on how well she has recovered from the birth. But you can make the environment very conducive to starting again. So take control of your baby and your partner will take control of you.

When to say I Love You

As a father, you can never say "I love you" too much to your child. Three such simple and short words can have such a deep and profound meaning in a parents' relationship with their child.

It is very important that you start straight away when your baby first comes into this world. As he grows up, because he has always heard you saying it to him, and he knows you mean it, he will always feel secure and stable in the knowledge that he is loved unconditionally by you and his mother.

Chapter 4

Help Me – He's A Toddler

Well, you made it through those early months and now you have the Toddler years to look forward to. These can be really fun years as your child grows and develops. He will look up to you and learn very quickly from you, whether it is how to hit a ball, ride a bicycle, or learn nursery rhymes. His brain is like a sponge and everything you do will be observed and taken in. Sometimes you will only realise exactly what he has registered when you are least expecting it. So be ready to be surprised.

Steve Biddulph, in his book 'How to Raise Boys', says that the mother is the most important point of reference for your child during these early years. This may seem to be the case, but don't let it put you off. I believe you are both as important as each other, only in different ways.

These initial years can have a huge impact on the closeness of your relationship with your child later on. Trust, respect, and love is built up during these early years, and all of these will help you overcome the challenges that lie ahead as they grow up. They will allow you to be truly involved with your child and be able to offer a balanced upbringing to him. You will never be a peripheral figure to your child, and together with your partner, you will be taking just as important role as she does. Remember, you as his father also have a duty to be involved in every aspect of his life.

The few years when your child is a toddler can be very tiring and stressful high energy stuff. They are so inquisitive and want to discover so much, and so quickly, but their attention span is very short. Beware, they can be a danger to themselves without you watching over them. When you couple your toddler's naivety and inexperience with their sudden energy spurts you have to balance the need to let them discover and explore life, with the need to keep them safe from themselves.

These are also really fun times, as you and your partner are the total centre of your child's universe. This is a huge responsibility as you are your Toddler's idol, role model, comforter, play mate, provider, and protector. However, the sense of satisfaction and joy for you, not to mention for your child, during these years as you build closer and closer bonds is nothing short of incredible.

When the inevitable challenges of bringing him up present themselves, which they inevitably will, hopefully you will feel that you have some potential options and solutions. And trust me, there will definitely be some occasions where you feel you need some.

<u>Stay one step ahead of your Toddler at night time</u>

From the day when your child first goes into her own room with her own cot or bed you need to be thinking about staying one step ahead. It will be a constant battle as she goes through this part of her childhood, and you need to be up to the task. So immediately put a gate up across the doorway. This will make sure she knows that she has to stay there until you or her mother come and bring her out in the morning.

How would you like an extra half an hour's sleep in bed in the morning? It can be so tiring and intense when your toddler is awake, whether it is at the end of the day, or at 5.00 am in the morning, finding a way to get that little extra time to sleep can be priceless. This technique really works. Once she is asleep, go into her room, and remove all the toys which are in there. Then replace them with a set of new toys which she hasn't played with for a week or so.

She will be fascinated when she wakes up and the new toys will keep her occupied, quiet, and give you and your partner an extra lie in the next morning. No more crying out 'mummy' or 'daddy', although you might vaguely hear her playing if you do wake up. This extra time for you and your partner to relax will be priceless for the first three or four years. It will also allow you to have a higher quality relationship with both your partner and your child, because you will not be so tired when you wake up. A good night's sleep makes everyone feel better.

Life Jacket

Change your child's toys every night, so when she wakes up early, she finds something new to play with.

Once you have got your Toddler into bed, don't close his bedroom door, leave it open! Many children can be afraid of the dark for no reason at all. Therefore, it will be reassuring for him if he wakes up in the middle of the night and doesn't feel cut off from the rest of the family. Pitch blackness can be very intimidating and scary for a young child.

In any case, most young children do not need complete darkness to sleep. When they are tired they will sleep anywhere, even in bright sunlight. How many times have you seen a small child fast asleep in his parent's arms in the middle of the day? It can also be a good discipline for later on in life. It may well help keep your child with an 'open' attitude to you and others, as he grows older. Hopefully, it will help avoid him trying to always close himself off in his bedroom when he is a teenager, and distancing himself from the rest of the family. It's amazing how something as simple and unscientific as this can help promote good habits later on in life. And these habits die very hard in later years.

I always found that our children didn't need silence to sleep. Young children sleep if they are tired, and if they are not, then they don't. It can be reassuring for your young child to hear normal family background noise when they go to sleep, so they do not feel cut off at bed time. It also means that your family can continue its normal household (sometimes noisy) routines in the evening. It is very important for your child's development that she is raised in as normal household environment as possible. It goes without saying that normality is relative, and based on your particular religion and culture.

A little night light in the background, particularly when your child is very young, will prevent her becoming afraid of the dark. Because she has this light on, as she grows older, darkness should never become an issue for her.

Life Jacket

Always leave a light on in the bathroom at night. This will reassure your child if she wakes up before daybreak.

When you tuck your Toddler in at night, always kiss him 'goodnight', and when you go and greet him the next day, kiss him 'good morning' as well. If you do this from birth it will become second nature to you both. It is yet another little brick in the castle of emotional ties that you are building up with your child, which will stay with both of you for life. Even if your child is asleep when you do this, subconsciously he will know and sense you have done it. It will also allow you both to close off the old day, and start an exciting new one together the next morning.

This habit will last all the way through to adulthood, and if you happen to forget one night, you can be sure your child will remind you. I once had an embarrassing episode with my daughter while I was taking an evening phone call from a potential new employer. I had answered the call before I had kissed her goodnight. She was 3 years old at the time.

I was downstairs trying to sell myself for a particular new job that I wanted and she was standing at the gate to her room shouting "kiss me goodnight Daddy". I could hear her very clearly, but was trying to remain focussed on the call. Eventually, having been distracted for about 15 minutes, the call was about to end, and the person interviewing me said "next time you should say goodnight to your child before you do a phone call like this". I was shocked as I thought she couldn't hear my Toddler. I then stumbled out some lame excuse, about why I hadn't said goodnight to my daughter yet, before saying goodbye to my interviewer. I didn't get the job by the way, so be warned.....

Life Jacket

Don't forget to kiss your child Goodnight, every night, or do so at your peril.

Eventually, the tables will be turned, and it will become normal for your child to kiss you goodnight! This is highly likely, particularly when he is older and going to bed much later than you! The first time this happens is quite a strange feeling, but you will get used to it. I will talk more about this 'role reversal' in a later Chapter.

As I said at the beginning of this book, there is no scientific evidence in what I suggest here, because these recommendations are based entirely on my own experiences raising my children.

Keeping your Toddler out of trouble during the day?

Your child will never refuse to play games with you, unless he is really under the weather. You must always play with your child and invent games which you can play together when you are at home. When he is very young, maybe only 2 years old, it could start with something as basic as a game of pointing to things as you call out its name. Or maybe you just ask your child to tell you what colour a particular item is. These are educational as well as good fun for your Toddler, as he will be learning what things are called and hearing how you pronounce various words.

When your child is old enough to support her own body weight, and hold on to you, let her ride around on your back, as if she is on a horse. If you have more than one child, get your partner to let the other one ride on her as well. Your children will love being 'jockeys', and it will teach them to balance and control their own body. You will love it as well, although your knees might not! But the pain is worth it when you see the look on your Toddlers face.

If you have a pet, who by now will be very used to your Toddler, it is a good opportunity for you to help your child feel confident around animals. This way he will learn to build relationships with a living creature which is not a human being. He will learn that the relationship between himself and a dog or another domestic pet is very different to the one he has with you, his mother or any siblings. This will help develop his respect for animals and his points of reference for later on in life.

Life Jacket

Encourage your child to respect and play with the family dog or pet.

When disciplining your Toddler is a real challenge

The easy option to get your child to comply with your request when he is naughty is to smack him. However, this will set a very negative precedent and send totally the wrong message to him that this is an acceptable way to resolve things. It uses fear and violence to achieve a result, and can be a very dangerous road to go down. There will be times when you are driven to distraction by your child and smacking becomes very tempting, but resist the urge, and step back. Much easier said than done, I know.

Try to use reason to resolve discipline issues with your Toddler, although this will be very challenging. Sit him down, try not to shout, as you risk losing your cool if you do, and explain to him firmly why his behaviour is unacceptable and why he should comply with your request. He needs to understand that you are very unhappy with the situation and there will be consequences if he does not do as he is told (easier said than done I know). Because he is so young, if he sees that you are 'angry' with him, he will not like this reaction from you or feel comfortable with it, and he will eventually understand that he is the cause of your anger, and his behaviour must change. But make no mistake, this is a real challenge.

I was once told this by a very successful MD of a Leadership company "One of the things that paralyses me most as a dad, is the fact that I can engage and inspire a Board of Directors to change the culture of their business, yet I can't inspire my 3 year old to put his shoes on!" This just emphasises how difficult it can be to manage a Toddler's behaviour. Patience, tolerance and perseverance are three skills that you will need bundles of during these years!

The Infamous Naughty Step

Somewhere to send your Toddler in complete safety will be a true 'godsend' during these years. I know from harsh experience. It seems such a basic idea, and one which I never even thought of before someone else told me. Luckily, after a few months of wondering how to manage a naughty Toddler, and not knowing quite what to do, a cousin of mine who has older children than mine suggested it. Thank goodness someone told me about this strategy, I dread to think how long it would have taken me to come up with the idea myself. After that, it helped resolve many a frustrating situation from exploding, and calmed things down in the family.

As a guide, and it only really works well up to 5 years old, if she is naughty, she has to sit of the lowest step of the stairs (below the stair gate of course) for 1, 2 or 5 minutes, depending on the severity of the 'offence'! It will feel like an age for your Toddler, but will be very effective. If you do not have a staircase, then use a box turned upside down, or a mini chair, in the corner of the living room. The fact that she has to stay in one place and not get up, even if only for a minute, will be a very effective deterrent. At the best of times, a young child finds it difficult to sit still, so imagine how difficult this will be for your child to comply. It really works.

By being sent to the Naughty Step your child will understand that she has done something wrong, and realise that this is a punishment for her behaviour. Initially, it may be like a game, but once she has been sent there a few times, and not been allowed to get off until the time is up, she will realise that it really is a punishment, and encroaches on her freedom. This is also a good time to introduce the concept of saying sorry, particularly after she has been on the Naughty Step for a few minutes. She will soon understand that if she says sorry she may get her punishment reduced.

Lifebuoy

Create the 'naughty step'. Once your child starts to be mobile, it will come in very handy.

When your Toddler is being very naughty and throwing a tantrum he will sometimes tell you that "he doesn't want to live here anymore", or "he hates you or his mother". If he says something like this, gently but firmly escort him to his room. Tell him that if he hates everyone or doesn't like living at home any more, then he doesn't have to.

Help him pack his little suitcase, recommending what he will need when he is no longer at home, and once his suitcase is full, walk him slowly to the front door, and then open it for him. You will see that he will progressively become more sheepish as this episode unfolds, and as you open the door, he will eventually apologise and say he doesn't really want to go. He will certainly be very well behaved for a few weeks after that, particularly if you remind him of it.

Lifebuoy

Don't be afraid to call your child's bluff when he is having a tantrum.

Getting Better quality of life at home with your Toddler

Even if you are exhausted when you arrive home from work, and you feel you don't have enough energy to have a little playtime with your child, force yourself to make that extra special effort. Always say hello to your child, wherever he is in the house, and listen to what he has to say to you about his day. It will be time very well spent, he will always want to greet you when you have been away, and he will remember the effort you made for him in later years.

It will also give your partner a break, and she will really appreciate the effort you have made. Even though she knows you are very tired from being out all day, the fact that you have made that special effort to relieve her will reap 'special' dividends for your relationship together. It will give her instant relief from the pressure of children, and it will definitely improve your sex life. This may seem like a wild claim but as she will be far more relaxed when she goes to bed it will definitely be more rewarding than if she is exhausted. It's a bit like knocking over a set of dominoes. You relieve the pressure on her, she spends time on herself, she relaxes, you get tired from playing with your Toddler, she spends time on you, you feel better, she feels better……it's a win/win situation……

The 'Best and Worst' Game

Now I am coming to one of the best discoveries I ever made during the whole of our children's upbringing. It is called the 'Best and Worst' game, which I would strongly recommend you to start as soon as your child is able to speak fully. Then you can develop and encourage this process while your child grows as a Toddler. Get into the habit of doing this at meal times, every day, and without fail. You will learn so much about your child's day, and your child will learn so much about your lives as well. By doing this simple exercise at the dinner table in the evening it will help reveal many things which are happening to your child (both positive and negative) during his daily life. It will be a real learning experience that brings you closer as a family and encourages constant open communication between you all.

Over the years, this simple routine at meal times could uncover such things as bullying at school, special achievement awards, or friendship and relationship problems, as well as many other things. We found out a lot of things that were happening at school, some good and a few bad, which we would never have known about so promptly if we hadn't had this routine every day. As a result of having found out about them quickly, we were able to get them resolved before they became bigger and more serious issues.

One evening while we were eating supper together, we started the 'Best and Worst' game. It was the turn of my eldest son. He started talking about the worst part of his day and said, "because I'm half French, everyone keeps calling me Froggie, or Snail. I really don't like it and it upsets me. I hate it, but when I tell people to stop, they just call me more names". It was really upsetting for my son and affecting his School work, but we did eventually find out about it at the dinner table. The next day my wife spoke to the School and they got all the children together. It was explained how name calling could be very hurtful, which the other children understood, and it stopped that day. We saw a real difference in our son's demeanour after that.

Not only will it end up keeping you closer to your children, and therefore always in the loop about what is happening in their lives, but it allows them to know what is happening in yours. As a father, who is very often away during the day working, your children will be interested to understand and know about your life as well. They love to 'know what Daddy does' and you will certainly want to know what they get up to!

A really special time for the whole family to be together on a daily basis is at meal times, as it will encourage high quality communication between you and your child. To improve the closeness of your family unit, always try to eat meals together, at least once a day if possible. Normally, this will be supper time, although breakfast is a good time at weekends. If you start doing this when your Toddler is very young it will be considered the normal thing to do. If you always use it as an opportunity to talk as a family together, many problems and challenges that present themselves to you over the years can be resolved quicker and easier. It will build high quality relationships between you, your partner and your child, as well as any siblings.

Sometimes, your child may take ages to eat, or maybe he is a real challenge to get to eat all his food at meal times. A strategy you could use is to ban him from talking until he has finished his food. Because he is so young, he will probably not question why he cannot talk, and won't think about any consequences if he doesn't comply. Despite there never being a threat of a punishment, he may well just do as he is told and eat all his food up in a reasonable time. When he is older, both of you will laugh at this, as the ridiculous thing is that there was never any sanction if he did talk!

We used this tactic very successfully with our youngest son who was a real chatterbox. We introduced this strategy at meal times and it worked right up to the age of 7, when 'the proverbial penny dropped'. He just would never stop talking at the table during a meal, as he was so desperate to tell everybody about what he had been doing during his day. But after 3 years of having to do this, he was much better and eating normally. So the problem was resolved. We laugh about it now as he still cannot believe that he complied with this for so long.

Isn't it annoying how often young children don't like eating food that is good for them, but love food that isn't? So it is very important that you

encourage your child to eat plenty of vegetables at a very early age. If he
sees that you do not eat cabbage or greens, as he copies so much of what
you do, he will assume that this is the correct way to behave. If he really
doesn't like something, start with very small portions and offer incentives
for 'eating all his vegetables up'. Eventually he will be happy to do this
and it will become normal for him. But you may need to persevere with
this, as it can take some time for your child to acquire the taste.

Reading together with your child is a great way of spending close, intimate
and relaxed moments with her, which both of you will love. These are
actually very special moments which are just shared between the two of
you. So try and read story books with your child as soon as she starts
talking, at around 18 months. Take every opportunity to do this during the
day, and always at bedtime. To help her learn while she is listening to you,
point to the words with her while you are doing it. Before this age, you can
sing songs to her when she goes to bed. In fact, you can still sing songs
with her after reading a story as she gets older. She will never complain.

It is really important that you, as her father do this, as well as her mother,
even if you think you sing terribly. Remember, to her, your voice is one of
the two most wonderful sounding voices in the world. This can last for as
long as you both enjoy it, and as she grows a bit, she can sing to you before
she goes to sleep. This is very high quality father/child time, both singing
and reading together, and will be enjoyed and remembered by both of you
for many years to come.

'Make Believe' is magical for your child

Christmas and New Year is the most magical time of year, and one for the
whole family to really enjoy being together. For your children, having
Daddy around helping Mummy prepare for Christmas, and sharing in the

excitement as it builds, will be very special. If you can, try to make sure you always spend Christmas and New Year with your children. You will see, that by always making an effort to be together at this time of year, when they are very young and as they grow older, they will want to continue to spend the Festive period with you. They will come to expect this, and it will always be like that, even when they have their own family unit. The tables might be turned though, and it will be them doing all the work.

Something you could do to make the magic of Father Christmas more realistic, is to dress up on Christmas morning, and very early, run across the lawn (or across a corridor if you live in an apartment) in your outfit. While you do that, your partner can call your child to the window or the door, so he can just manage to catch a glimpse of Father Christmas disappearing round the side of the building. While your child is still looking on in disbelief, you can quickly come inside, get rid of your outfit, join in and share in the amazement. Your child will be convinced he has seen Santa Claus.

Lifebuoy

Make sure you don't wear your normal shoes though, or ones which your Toddler can recognise.

Always keep in mind when you decide to do this that your Child is extremely observant. One year I forgot to put boots on, and wore a pair of my everyday shoes. When I got back inside the house all pleased with my little charade, my son asked very 'matter of factly' why Father Christmas was wearing my shoes. Fortunately, he was still very young, only 2 years old, and I was able to explain it away by saying lots of people had shoes like mine. It wouldn't have worked if he had been much older.

Routine for your Toddler will make your life easier

Regulate bedtimes from an early age, right up to the age of 16 which should be, as a guideline, 10.00pm. 15 Minutes extra should be given for every birthday reached. For example, at age 4, your child's bedtime should be 7.00 pm, or at 13, it will have progressed to 9.15pm. Start this as soon as he goes to school, when he is 4 or 5 years old. By doing this from such an early age and sticking to it rigorously, bedtimes and going to bed will never become a controversial issue. It is considered non-negotiable and as a result everyone complies without question.

Once you have established this routine in your child's life, introducing a system of giving him 15 minutes warning before bedtime will make your life even easier. This will allow him to finish the game he is playing, or the TV program he is watching and be ready to go to bed on time. This way, he will not argue with you once his bedtime has arrived. Another benefit for you and your partner, is that you will always know that you can relax a bit together at a certain time in the evening, once your child has gone to bed.

Life Jacket

Regulate bedtimes from an early age, it will make your life easier.

Make it a special celebration for every birthday in the family for you, your partner and your children. You can do this by all going out for a meal together. It could be a fast food meal, or a meal in a restaurant, depending on your budget. But for one day a year, each member of the family has one day where you celebrate it all together. For that day, the 'Birthday Boy or Girl' is the most important person in the family, and is spoilt by everyone else. Your child will love being treated like this and being made to feel so special during the entire day. You will love it too.

The simplest way to keep your kids happy in the car

A good game that you can play with your Toddler in the car is 'the snooker game'. Ask your child to spot the colours of cars in the order of the balls played in a game of snooker. You start with white, then a red, then yellow, and all the way up to black. Have you ever noticed how few yellow, brown or pink cars there are? In fact, there are hardly any pink ones at all. You can keep this game going for as long as you need to. If you want to make it last longer, you can insist that after each red car is spotted, you have to spot another white one again before you can choose a coloured one. It will keep your child amused for ages, as well as distracting you.

Another game you can play is looking for the type or make of car. For example, a Volkswagen Beetle, or an Aston Martin DB9. If you want the game to last a little longer for your child then choose a rare type of car. If you want your child to find it quickly, choose a more popular model. There are many variations on this theme that you can use depending on how creative you want to be. For example, it could be colours, or marques of lorries, buses, vans or even caravans and trailers.

If you prefer to do more educational games with your child you can play 'Capital cities of the world'. This game is both interesting and educational, for you and your child, and keeps him focussed on fun learning instead of getting frustrated because he is bored in the car. Start with very easy ones such as the Capital city of England or Scotland. You call out the country, and your child has to guess its Capital city. Once he gets used to and starts to learn some of the answers, then you can progress to other more difficult ones from European or South American countries. You will be amazed just how much knowledge your child will pick up and retain.

Lifebuoy

Play games in the car to stop your child getting bored and agitated. It will make the time go much quicker.

As you know, the car can be a very challenging environment with your small child, so keeping him happy is a real challenge. So once you have exhausted all the previous games options, you can start singing songs together. This will work well for you, and can be used as a means of passing time between two points on the road. If it is fifteen minutes until your exit, you can devise a game for all of you to sing songs one after the other, and you can all give marks out of ten to everyone else. For example, between two junctions on a Motorway, suggest to everyone in the car to sing an agreed song or nursery rhyme until the second junction is reached. There must be no exceptions, and everyone must join in. Let your child choose the song as soon as the one you chose is finished.

You will see that time passes very quickly when you do this, and it is very good for strengthening bonds between you and your child. It also reinforces your child's sense of doing fun things with you. Remember you want to have really good fun with your child, and that this is a very important part of your everyday relationship. For example, while going under the Dartford or the Mersey Tunnel, you and your child could sing "10 little ducks went swimming one day". The goal would be to finish the song exactly when you leave the tunnel. Your child will be enthralled.

Inventing stories to tell to your child in the car can be totally captivating for him. For example, you could invent a story about 'The Wicked Witch of Gott' (this is a totally made up name by the way). She is an old witch who sits at her window watching the children go to school. If somebody pulls a face at her, she will cast a spell and the face will remain permanent on the child who pulled it. The only way to get your normal face back is if you apologise to the Witch in person (nobody wants to do that, because she is so scary). Only then can you get your normal facial expression back. You can adapt this story with different characters, and draw it out or shorten it depending on the length of time you are in the car.

Not only will this be great fun, but it will subconsciously be teaching your child to be polite, not to pull faces at people, and respect others who are different from them.

Your child will love stories which are told by you, so you can be very creative with them. For example, you could invent one about a family of dinosaurs and its prehistoric adventures, with each dinosaur representing one member of your family. You can let your Toddler choose who is what dinosaur, then you can recount a story which you can make up as you go along. If you let your child choose who you are, you might find you always end up being the Brontosaurus. To this day, I still haven't worked out why this was always the case, as I always wanted to be a Tyrannosaurus Rex.

I have written a few more ideas on different stories and games you can do to amuse your Toddler, which you can find in the Appendix at the back of this book.

<u>Your Toddler and your childhood</u>

Your child will love to hear about your childhood, so hearing about what you did when you were young will fascinate him. Tell him what games you used to play, particularly the ones you used to invent. It will captivate him listening to stories about what you got up to when you were his age. However, make sure the stories you tell are true and relevant to his age group as a Toddler. Also be careful only to tell him things that you would be happy for him to get up to, as he will definitely try to copy what you did.

It is good that when your child is a Toddler, she can learn about objectives and what can happen if she achieves them. She needs to understand that when they are reached, they produce benefits. If she puts all her toys away at the end of the day before going to bed, then she will be able to have an extra 5 minutes in the bath. She will love this, and will respond very positively to it.

An interesting experiment to play with your child is 'The Marshmallow Test'. The book of the same name by Walter Mischel elaborates around this concept. This will help your child learn and understand the concept of waiting for a reward depending on her behaviour. It is also an exercise in self-control. Give her a marshmallow first, then explain that if she waits to eat it for 10 minutes, she will get a second one. If she opts to eat it immediately she will only get one. It will be interesting for you to see how she reacts. Also, it will certainly reveal a few instinctive traits of character that she has.

A friend of mine, James, did this with his two children many years ago when they were Toddlers, and it is interesting to see how they responded, and how their character has developed today, now they are adults. The one who ate his immediately has quite a 'short fuse', and is impatient to get things done. He really responds to goal setting. The other one, who waited 10 minutes for a second marshmallow, is very laid back and reserved. It's not scientific, but it is very interesting to observe. Try it. I'm sure you will find it a revealing exercise to do with your children. I did it with my three and the results were true to character as well.

Life Jacket

Set goals for your Toddler, which are achievable for her, and that yield a tangible reward.

When something doesn't go the way your Toddler wants it to, his instinct may be to start sulking. This can be very frustrating for everyone, so you have to try to encourage him not to do it. This is very important, because as he grows up, he will come across many things that don't go his way. As a Toddler, his first instinct will be to start sulking. This is fine when he is at this age as he still needs to learn, but if he resorts to sulking when he is older he may lose friends or opportunities, which could have a profound effect on his achievements in life.

When your child starts the inevitable sulk, when things haven't gone his way, try to distract him by talking about or doing something he loves. This will teach him that there is always the next positive thing or opportunity happening which he enjoys doing. This will help him learn to move on from the previous disappointment. When he is old enough to listen to reason, around 4 to 5 years old, you can then explain to him why sulking is such a poor social skill to have, and reinforce this message on a regular basis.

If your child has a tendency to cry when he doesn't get what he wants, use the distraction technique as well. It works on the same principle as when your child sulks. It is important that you try to avoid having a child who always cries when he doesn't get his own way. Nobody likes a 'cry baby'!

Sensitivity is also an important part of your child's psychological development. It will help her manage many situations that she comes across in life, but beware of her being over sensitive, as this can be a real problem for her in later years. It is therefore very important that she learns to manage this behaviour during her childhood. You as her father should lead by example, and show that you can be sensitive to other people's feelings, but never become over sensitive to them and end up getting upset. You need to keep everything in perspective, and lead by example with your Toddler, and she will follow.

Annabelle's Massive Nose

Your child is very observant and is constantly soaking up so much of his surrounding environment. He has very acute hearing and eyesight, and will pick up any loose words or actions you may say or do. If you make an 'off the cuff' comment about someone, make sure you say it out of earshot of your child, or it could come back to haunt you with a vengeance.

When my oldest child was about 3 years old I made the mistake of commenting on the appearance of one of our friends. It became one of the most embarrassing moments I ever experienced in relation to our social life. After our friend's wedding, we were watching a short video that we had taken of it, before we were going to offer it to them. My son was in the room playing with his toys, so I didn't think at all about him listening to what we were saying. While we were watching the video, there was a certain camera angle shot which made our friend's nose look very big. I made an 'off the cuff' remark to my wife, "I didn't realise that Annabelle had such a big nose", and I thought nothing more of it until the next day, when Annabelle came round to our house.

No sooner had she stepped inside the house, when my son shouted out "Daddy says you have a big nose"! I almost died of embarrassment on the spot. I tried to say that my son was saying 'be noise', or an invented word 'benose', but to no avail. As I was saying this, my son kept on saying very loudly "no Daddy, you said big nose". That day became the start of the end of our friendship.

Life Jacket

Be careful what you say in earshot of your Toddler, it may come out when you are least expecting it.

Chapter 5

Help - She's Growing Up

During these years, there are new challenges to be faced as a father. Your children, by now, will be looking up to you consciously as their role model. Everything that you do will be closely watched and copied by your child. Therefore, you need to be very careful what you say and do and how you behave generally. Remember they will be looking more and more towards you for guidance on how you interact with them, other people and society in general. It is therefore very important that you behave in a responsible and appropriate manner at all times.

You only have one chance to make a first impression

A key social skill your child needs to learn at a very early age is to always positively greet people when he meets them. He should greet the person you are/he is meeting with a firm handshake (if you have a boy) and a kiss (if you have a girl). He should also be encouraged to look people in the eye when he is saying hello to them. This will be very useful in creating a good first impression with new people as he grows up. Remember, we only ever have one chance to make a first impression. He should be encouraged to embrace this approach to other people, as he will use it for the rest of his life.

To help promote good manners and effective communication skills, your child should always make your visitors feel welcome in your home. When they arrive at your house, make sure your children always get up from whatever they are doing and come and say hello to them. Whatever they are doing or wherever they are, you should encourage them to come and greet your guests. This will promote good manners, help them with effective communication skills, and will always make your visitors feel welcome in your home. It will also help make them positive outward going individuals, which is a great social skill and which other people will value, as they grow up into adulthood.

Life Jacket

Encourage your children wherever they are in the home to positively come and greet guests and make them feel welcome.

Encourage your child not to be afraid to talk to strangers (only in your company though, while they are under 16). They should always see and treat people as their equals, while at the same time always being respectful of them. Just because they are a child doesn't mean they are inferior to someone else, despite what some adults still believe. This will make them confident individuals as they grow older. But, of course, you can only start this interaction with them when they are old enough to adequately hold a conversation with another individual and appreciate 'stranger danger'.

<u>Avoiding a shouting match.</u>

Make sure you always stay calm (much easier said than done, but with practice it is possible), as you will always react better to a situation if you are calm. If you allow yourself to get angry with your child it will just become a shouting match. It will degenerate on both sides and you will both become even more frustrated and may then end up saying and doing things that you will both regret later.

If your child can't get a reaction from you and he realises that you are very calm, he will soon understand that you are always in control of the situation and therefore more likely to achieve what you want. The good thing is that on the very odd occasion when you really do become angry, your child will know how rare this is and will more than likely back off immediately. This way, your 'controlled anger' will always have more impact and be more effective and again help you achieve your objective. You need to ensure that you are consistent at all times however. Stick to your guns if you believe you are right.

Life Raft

If your child is pushing you and you feel your anger is rising and you might 'lose your cool', step away from the situation quickly and count to 10.

Of course, sometimes you will be in the wrong and your child will know this. The key word then is 'sorry', which I mentioned right at the beginning of this book. Used wisely and sincerely, it will help you resolve many situations which haven't gone as planned and get you out of some very difficult and degenerating circumstances. With children, there is no room for pride. If you are in the wrong, just admit it and move on. This is also a good life lesson for them to learn.

Growing up in the blink of an eye.

Keep your child believing in the Tooth Fairy and Father Christmas for as long as possible. Even though your child is growing up, let him take his time and don't make him grow up too fast. That will come soon enough. Childhood is magical and 'make believe' forms an integral and exciting part of it pre-puberty. From time to time, try to do something exceptional to keep your child believing.

For example, this was a strategy that I used and that worked very well for my children. You could prepare your action by saying that you would never ever have a Games Console in the house, as you hate them so much. But then, as a total surprise and without being consulted, 'Father Christmas' could bring your child one on Christmas morning. This will be so convincing, that even though your child may have serious doubts whether Father Christmas exists, through school friends or TV, he will continue to believe for a little longer. If it is your oldest child, he will certainly keep the magic going a bit longer for both him and his younger siblings.

Your child knows you really are human.

Always be interested in what your child is doing in her life. After all she came from you, is part of you and will always be interested in what you do. Even though sometimes she will say she isn't. It is important to remember that the relationship between you and your child is evolving all the time as she grows up. It is very dynamic and throws up new challenges almost every day. By being fully aware of and interested in what she is doing, you can evolve with her as your relationship develops together over time.

As their Father, your children will always be interested in you sharing your successes with them. It doesn't matter if it is at work or on the sports field, or anywhere else in life. By doing this, your children will always feel that you are treating them as an equal and so will be interested in what you do. It will also become normal routine that you share with each other what life throws up at you. They will also want to share your failures, not because they want you to fail, but because it will confirm to them that you are human. They know you are anyway, but sometimes they need to hear you telling them why you are.

If you can, try to go and watch their sports matches, their concerts or their school plays as often as you can. For them this is very important and demonstrates your commitment to them. They know you work hard, but still you are prepared to make the effort to support them. It shows you are interested in what they do and that you really care. It makes you relevant to their everyday lives and allows you to share in their achievements. In later years, if you have done this, it will help you both manage any situation that arises as they grow up because you have so many shared experiences. This will be particularly important during the challenging teenage years to come, but because you have always shared all these important moments with them, you will get through them together.

Dads can play in the mother's netball match!

Your child will love the fact that his father has made the effort to play against him at school. If you can, play as many father's sports matches against your child as possible and even take the odd half-days holiday from work to do this. He will be so proud of you and of course you will be of him. It doesn't even matter if you are any good at sports, so long as you play, whether it is football, cricket or even netball.

I once played in a 'mother's netball' match against my daughter, as my wife was unexpectedly ill that day. She loved the fact I had made the effort and was happy to have a go, even though I didn't know any of the rules of the game. It didn't matter that I made a complete fool of myself and it really was very comical. The fact that I had done it for my daughter and made the effort, was what really mattered to her. She still recounts that match very fondly today and with lots of laughter, many years on.

One of the major responsibilities you have as a father is to give your child choices in her life. One of the ways you can do this is by encouraging your child to try everything, sport, music, art, dance etc. She will learn through experience and won't know what she will like or dislike until she has tried it. The only way your child can learn about these choices is by trying things and experiencing them. So encourage her in everything she tries. She will eventually find what works best for her and what she enjoys doing. Then she will usually go ahead and concentrate on that.

Encouraging your child to take responsibility for his actions and his life will help him understand the potential dangers that it can hold. For example, when he is about 6 or 7, if he has learnt to swim already, let him swim a little distance away from you. He will love this 'independence', and the fact that he is in control of what he is doing and you are not. Or if you go for a walk and find a tree, let him climb it. You could even climb it with him (if you can of course), as this allows you to be nearby should he need a little help.

Life Jacket

Let your child take calculated risks, but make sure he understands the dangers and consequences.

Accidents do happen

Try not to get worked up when your child breaks things. Rarely do children break things deliberately, usually it is an accident. If she does on the rare occasion, break something deliberately, then you have to take the appropriate action and punish her. But if it is an accident, explain that these things happen, and move on. You can then use it as an opportunity to positively reinforce good behaviour if she is a bit more careful next time. In life, accidents do happen, and in any case, material possessions can be replaced, so don't over dramatize things.

Make the punishment fit the crime

Your child's bedroom should be his special place where he always has good sentiments and feels secure. This should be the case all through his childhood. Always try to keep this in mind when you are considering punishing your child. Avoid ever sending your child to his bedroom as a punishment during the day, as this will make his room become synonymous with a negative experience and a place he is sent to when he is in trouble. As an alternative, you can always send him to bed early, as this is different, because the punishment is going to bed early, not being sent to his room.

Always make sure that the punishment fits the crime. If your child steals something from someone else, you should punish him strongly by withdrawing privileges. This could be no TV or Games for a week, but make sure the punishment is appropriate for the misdemeanour. If it is done correctly, it will teach your child a very strong lesson; never to steal again. He also needs to learn that certain behaviour is totally unacceptable. However, If you get it wrong, it may end up sending a completely different message to the one you want to get over. It is therefore very important to teach your child that there are always consequences for unacceptable behaviour.

Always say Sorry

This is one of the most important lessons you can teach your child as she grows up. If you have had a disagreement during the day, or are in the wrong, or even both of you are, always say sorry to each other. Also, never forget to kiss her goodnight before she goes to sleep, irrespective of whatever has gone on between you. By doing this simple act, it will ensure that no grudges or ill feelings are ever held onto overnight. Then tomorrow just becomes another new day. Forgive, forget and move on. Teaching her not to hold a grudge will help her hugely when she is an adult and help her focus on positive things in life and let go of any negative things.

Life Jacket

Forgive and forget, tomorrow is another day. Move on and don't ever bear a grudge.

Never disagree with your partner in front of your children

Very often it will happen that you don't agree with something that your partner has said or done with your children, or vica-versa. When this happens, resist the urge to say something that your children might interpret as a split between you, even if you really want to. Then once you and your partner are in private, you can express your disagreement with each other out of earshot.

If children can divide their parents (not literally), they know they are more likely to get away with something. If they manage to do this often, it might eventually, as they grow up, result in a lack respect for you and your partner's authority. Beware the subconscious 'Divide and Conquer' objective that your children have towards you and their mother. If they want to achieve a goal, which they know will be hard to convince both of you about, they will very often resort to this tactic.

Life Jacket

Never contradict your Partner in front of your children, even if you don't agree with her. Your children need to see their parents united and consistent all the time.

It's a contract so stick by it!

If you want certain rules followed by all your children, which are maybe being lost and ignored during everyday life in the home, draw up an 'Agreement' and include everyone in the family in it. Have the 'Agreement' signed by all the family members, so everyone is very clear what their individual obligations are. Clearly state on it what is required and by whom and then get everyone in the family to sign it to show their commitment to it. This will avoid arguments in the future as everyone is party to it. In the Appendix section at the end of this book, you will find an Example of one of these, 'The Hearn's Agreement'.

Positive incentives work

Always offer your children incentives for being good. This could be something like offering to take them on a day trip to the seaside if they put all their clothes away at bedtime for a whole month. Positive reinforcement will make them feel good about themselves, you and life generally. It will also encourage them to have a positive outlook on life, which will ultimately make them a happier person as they grow up.

Introduce a 'Good Star' system at home. Every week, create a little competition between your children and award stars to each of them. These are given for good behaviour or good deeds carried out by them. Then whoever gets the most stars at the end of the week receives a reward. This could be something special that they would really like to have, or do, such as a trip to see a new film at the cinema, or having their favourite Spaghetti Bolognaise for supper. We live in a competitive world and your children need to understand this concept throughout their daily lives .

When you are travelling in the car and are stuck in a traffic jam and your children are misbehaving, playing games together will help relieve the stress. These could be the same ones that you did when they were toddlers as they will still enjoy them (see previous chapter). But you can also do more educational games now they are a bit older, which are also good fun to play.

Get them to recite the 2 times table in one minute and offer them an incentive if they get it right within the time period. The incentive could be a sweet, or an extra minute before going to bed, or whatever you choose. By only offering a minute per correct times table, you are unlikely to be giving them too much extra time before going to bed. You and your partner still need your relaxing downtime when they are in bed, so don't give too much time away. As they get older it could be the 6 times or 9 times tables, depending on what age they are. The reward should always be something theyenjoy. It's more as a gesture really and not very expensive. After all, it is a game and they should know their times tables anyway. More examples of games to play in the car to amuse your children are included in the Appendix at the end of this book.

Rugby in the kitchen!

When the food shopping is ready to be put away get your children involved and make it fun. You could suggest passing things around the kitchen like in a rugby match, but make sure everyone playing the game is concentrating and can catch well. This will get the food from the shopping bag to their final places in a cupboard or a fridge, involving everyone in the family. One person empties the bags and other members of the family are positioned in front of their respective cupboards.

I was playing this game with my children once and got distracted by our dogs. I didn't stay focussed and watch what was going on and paid the price for it. I received a yoghurt pot on my head. Not only did it hurt a little, but I also enjoyed a new type of shampoo on my hair. The dogs loved cleaning it up though. Maybe it was a deliberate tactic by the children. Occasionally, an egg got dropped as well, but it was worth it, as everyone had great fun and the job got done with the whole family working together. The dogs enjoyed the odd accident as well.

Beware hidden dangers for your child

There is hidden danger lurking everywhere for your child and it is particularly risky after dark and beyond their bedtimes. Your children do not have the experience to know where danger is lurking, so you have to take this responsibility fully for them. Even if it is a hassle for you and you haven't got time. You must never forget this. Many of the accidents that befall children are totally avoidable, and as a Father and a Parent it is your number one responsibility to keep them safe.

Life Jacket

Remember your children are very young and vulnerable in these pre-teen years. It is very important that you are consistent and never let them roam outside on the streets or in public areas unsupervised and never after dark.

Be open and honest with your children

Never be afraid to show your emotions to your child. This is very important as it shows you are human and that certain things in life do affect you. Your child will respect you for doing this. It will also help him react appropriately to you depending on the situation. By showing your child that emotions are a normal and positive reaction to life situations, it will help him to develop his own emotional maturity as he grows up. He will be able to read the situation, then behave and respond appropriately to others and his surroundings.

Occasionally, a 'white lie' is acceptable, if it is done to protect your child from something. Particularly if they are not yet at an age when they can understand the full consequences of it. However, you should always try to be honest with your children, and never lie to them on serious issues. Sometimes it is very difficult to stick to this guideline, but remember that your children deserve you to treat them correctly. If, however, you do lie to them and they find out, it will send the message that this is an acceptable form of behaviour. Remember, at all times you have to be their role model, as they will copy a lot of what you do.

Chapter 6

<u>**Help - I've got a Teenager**</u>

When your children become teenagers the dynamics of your relationship change dramatically, so you need to evolve and become a different kind of role model. They will be mixing with a wide variety of individuals independently to you, and it is important that you remain consistent in how you behave towards them. 'Work hard … play hard', is a very important philosophy you need to get through to your teenager, and to do this you must lead by example.

As they will be trying new things during these years and following your example (where it suits them of course) try to avoid doing anything to excess yourself. While they need to understand that they can enjoy themselves, this must be linked to working hard, particularly at school. Therefore, they need to see the example of 'normal acceptable behaviour' coming from their father.

It is vitally important that your child feels he can still communicate with you openly while he is a teenager. So this will be one of your biggest challenges during the next few years. Therefore, keeping all lines of communication open between you both is vital, and will influence strongly how your relationship with him develops. However difficult and awkward the subject is, you can never have a 'bad conversation' with your child, only a good one, even if it doesn't feel like it at the time. With all the challenges facing him during this period of his life, this is where you will really benefit from the investment in time and effort you made with him during his earlier years.

It is during that period where you have laid the foundations, to allow you to stay connected during the extremely challenging times ahead of you. Your child is still very vulnerable when he is a teenager, but he neither believes nor realises this, and he will get sick of hearing you telling him this. He will be rebellious and very difficult to manage at times, so your role really is to guide him through this stage of his life. Don't worry, he will come out the other side, every child does, and hopefully with a sense of independence and respect for you and his mother, as well as other people. He will need this sense of value and perspective when he becomes an adult.

<u>Your Child's Role Model</u>

This is one of the most important things you can do as the father of a teenager. Lead by example: work hard, be nice to people, be consistent, respect others and their opinions, and be honest with yourself and your children (as well as others). Your child will be observing you very closely, although she may very often appear not to care at all what you are saying or doing.

As a role model for your teenager, you need to continue to pass on your life skills (only the good ones of course, even if your teenager quite likes some of your bad ones). These cover a wide variety of areas, such as social interaction with others, management of finances, and the need to work hard to achieve things in life.

An area that is very often ignored by parents is the development of personal Financial Management skills. This is absolutely vital for your child to learn as this life skill could have very serious implications, and even ruin your child's life when he is older. The importance of grasping an understanding first, and then managing this area of his life is a key life discipline.

You will need to make a real effort to teach your child this skill, and it should start when he becomes a teenager. He will by now be receiving pocket money from you, to buy the personal things he wants, some of which he cannot afford. You need to discuss with him about the concept of budgeting and managing how to balance his immediate need, with what he can afford. He needs to understand that he must save a portion of his weekly money until he has sufficient funds to buy what he wants. This is a very important message to get over to him, as it is very dangerous and potentially disastrous if he doesn't understand this concept when he becomes an adult.

Your child will already have an idea of what she is good at and what she isn't, and your job is to guide and encourage her. Always respond positively and always encourage her. This will give her belief in what she can achieve. You need to be a realist in terms of her ambitions, while at the same time never stifling her dreams. This is a very difficult balancing act to do, particularly as nearly all teenagers are full of self-doubt, not to mention the mood swings. If you get this balancing act right, you will launch your child into life with a very positive attitude, but if you get it wrong, it will make this transition much more challenging.

<u>No subject is taboo</u>

There must never be any subject that is taboo between you and your teenage child, no matter what it is. You should be able to talk to your son and daughter about any subject and not feel embarrassed (so should their mother by the way). Whether it is when to have sex for the first time or a first period, with your daughter, or a discussion about masturbation with your son. It may feel very awkward, but every subject must be able to be discussed openly.

The more open the communication links between you and your child, the higher quality, and more enjoyable your life with them will be. You will also be a much better father to them than if you avoid these things. The discussion may not always be an easy one to have with your child, but however difficult it is, always remember, it is a good conversation to have. Your child will respect you for trying to discuss a difficult subject, although at the time he may be just as embarrassed as you. This will give you strong credibility with him the older he gets. So if a crisis ever occurs, which it will at some point, he will feel comfortable accepting your help.

If there is a particular subject like excessive drinking, or drug taking that you want to discuss with your child, don't be afraid to raise it with them. Choose a relaxed moment, such as an evening meal, or late at night when you or your teenager is in bed. Then bring the subject up as if it was any routine subject you would chat to each other about. You can start it with an open ended question, such as "What do you think about alcohol, or drugs?"

This seems a very innocuous question, and the way you have asked it is neither controversial nor provocative. With this approach, your teenager will not feel threatened by your question and should respond to you. It may take a while, but as you are at the table eating and as the discussion progresses, you can probe deeper and pass your message in a positive way. But make sure that you are listening to what your child has to say on the subject all the time. If it becomes a monologue from you, with your ideas being stated all the time, there will be no meaningful conversation between you.

Life Jacket

You should never create any barriers to communication between you, however uncomfortable it is. Whatever the subject, it is always a good conversation.

Many times during these years you will come into conflict, or at least have disagreements with your child. Consequently, I would like to reiterate this point again, as it is just as relevant now as it was when your child was little. In these very sensitive and challenging times, never be afraid to say 'sorry' to your teenager if you get it wrong. It can sometimes be the hardest word you will ever have to say to your child, but always put misplaced pride aside and say it. If you are prepared to do this, it will really be appreciated by her, and she will realise that you recognise that you got something wrong and you admit it. Your children know already that you are not infallible, but sometimes they need to hear it from you. This will strengthen your relationship with them and the respect they have for you immeasurably.

Lifebuoy

Always be ready to say sorry if you are in the wrong and admit your mistake. On many occasions it will save a potentially disastrous situation from developing.

Grab that Drinks Coaster

Very often, when your children are teenagers they can be quite difficult to have a rational discussion with. As a result, the situation can degenerate quite quickly into a confrontation and a shouting match.

It was actually my youngest son who came up with this idea, and I think it is genius. It will make sure that both of you are listened to fully by the other one individually and that you have to actually listen to what each other is saying. Always keep a few drinks coasters around the house, they come in very handy in these situations, which can blow up anywhere and at any time.

If your child holds the coaster in her hand, then she can talk as much as she wants and as long as she wants, and you must listen without butting in. Once she has finished, she hands it over to you, and it is your turn to speak. You can then take as long as you want, and say whatever you want. The coaster can be passed between you both as often as you need to keep talking with each other. Not only will this calm you both down, but it will allow you both to say what you want to say, and prevent the situation escalating. It will save a lot of angry and nasty words from being exchanged, and keep some degree of civility between you both. Very often it will end up with you both smiling at each other, as you realise that the whole issue has been blown out of all proportion.

Life Raft

A good way to prevent a shouting match from happening is to use 'The Drinks Coaster Strategy'.

<u>Staying relevant to your Teenager</u>

Even though your child is now a Teenager, he still enjoys playing. It is important to make a constant effort every day and spend time playing with him. Whether it is kicking a football around, or playing on his Xbox. He will love this and really appreciate this quality time spent with you. It is also an opportunity for you to learn from him, particularly on the games console, as he will almost certainly be a lot better than you. If you both enjoy it, and you both will, these kind of activities can continue irrespective what age he is. It will help you understand more about what makes your child feel good when he is relaxing.

When you get in from having been out for the day, even if you are exhausted, always be prepared to make that extra effort for your child, like you have always done since she was very little.

Your partner may be too tired or is simply unable to help with your child's homework, and your child has convinced herself that she doesn't understand it. This is where she needs her Dad to step in and help get it sorted. Get your daughter to sit down with you and explain slowly what she needs you to do to help her. This will give you a couple of minutes to gather your breath having just got back home. It will also allow you to relax a bit. Your daughter will feel better as well, as she will feel you are in control of things.

To relax you and calm her down before you start, and to put her in a better mood, get her to quickly tell you what the best part of her day was. This will relax her and make her feel better and more positive. It will also give you a little more breathing space. Then you can start the homework. This will allow you to turn a stressful situation into a more relaxed one, and the problem nearly always will be solved quicker and easier. If she tries to resolve the issue when she is relaxed, she is far more likely to find the solution to her homework problem. You may even end up not actually doing anything, but simply being the facilitator and not the problem solver.

Lifebuoy

If you can see your child is stressing out, and she tells you she needs 'urgent help with her homework' as "Mummy can't do it", make this your number one priority. This is your opportunity to 'save the day' again.

Sharing and experiencing your child's proudest moments will be very rewarding for your both. For example, if your daughter is in a Talent Show at school, try to be there to see her perform. Or if she is in a Sports team and it is a special occasion such as a final, always make the effort to be present. In fact, even for regular school matches, you should try to support your child as often as possible. If her team loses and she doesn't do as well as she had hoped in the match, you will be there to support her through his disappointment. You can use situations like these to help your child understand and accept that in life you will not always succeed.

I always remember what my mother said to me when I was a child, and have used it so often with my own children. It is as true today as the first time I ever heard it. "If at first you don't succeed, try, try and try again".

This philosophy will help your teenager hugely in life, as she grows up and goes her own way. Tell her about things that didn't work out for you, and how you never gave up, but moved on and achieved something different. For example, it could have been a University which rejected your degree application, or an unsuccessful job interview. But you ended going to a different place and had an amazing time there anyway. Some things just don't go to plan and work out differently to how you wanted and imagined it. Your child needs to understand that life can be like this.

Lifebuoy

By doing things together you will reinforce the bonds between you and make them even stronger. Activities which both of you enjoy doing will help keep you close during these teenage years. For example, if you have a son who loves fishing, make the effort to spend time doing it with him, even if it is only once every three months. Or if you have a daughter who loves singing, do karaoke with her. It doesn't matter whether or not you are any good at fishing or singing. Your child will love the fact you are making the effort, and in fact, so will you. This will help you both when you end up in a potential conflict situation, which happens very often with teenagers, and because of that closeness it will allow you on many occasions, to find an acceptable solution to it.

Goals focus efforts

It is important that your child learns and understands the principle that work and effort will yield rewards in all areas of his life and that goals will focus his efforts.

For example, you could incentivise your child on the GCSE grades he achieves. If they are all A's or A*'s, the reward could be £5 or £10 per grade, or whatever figure you feel is most appropriate. Alternatively, you might offer to buy him some nice clothes for when he starts his 'A' levels. When he actually takes his 'A' levels you could even have other rewards, like going on a special family holiday together, somewhere he has always wanted to go to. It doesn't have to be an expensive reward, but it should be meaningful to him. The rewards can of course be different, but they should always be worth making the effort for.

If you like the concept of Pocket money, it can be increased for every birthday that is reached, although it is only really needed once your child becomes a teenager. How much it increases every year is entirely for you to decide, but I suggest increasing it by 50p per week. You should resist the temptation (and emotional pressure from your child) to just give him money as his 'god given right'. Make sure he understands that it is linked to effort. If he does the household chores he is expected to do on time, then he is learning that he has to 'earn' it.

This is good grounding for when he goes to work later on in life. If he doesn't work hard at his job, he won't be paid, so if he doesn't do what has been agreed around the house, then he simply won't receive his pocket money for that week.

Your teenager always needs money to buy certain things which he wants, and you need to keep this in mind. When you are setting the jobs which need to be done around the house, make sure they are meaningful and contribute to the daily running of your home. Your child may want to buy such things as computer games, fashion clothes, make-up, or simply want to go out with his friends to the cinema etc. This is where the basic Financial Management principles that you will have been teaching him, will come in very useful. Some things he will be able to buy immediately, but other things he will have to save up and wait for.

Your Teenager is teaching you

If you can learn to appreciate your teenager's environment, such as his tastes in clothes, as well as his music, it will be a good start. It is very important to avoid driving a wedge between you and your child particularly at this stage of his life. Although you may not approve of some of his friends, while you can tell him discreetly about your concerns, you have to let him make his own decisions. He will discover on his own later on, whether he has made good decisions or not. If you can do this it will keep you much closer to him when problems arise.

Keeping relevant means making a real effort to keep up with your teenagers' technology, his games and his music. You should learn to play his computer games with him and get him to teach and explain things to you. He will love the fact that he can teach you things as well, and it is not always the other way round. By having this approach you will always stay an integral part of his life, as he evolves through his teenage years. Although on many occasions it won't feel like it at all and it won't stop the arguments and disagreements, he will definitely respect you for trying to do this.

Whatever your child is up to, positive feedback about what he is doing will always be well received by him. Even if you actually disagree with what he is actually doing. During this period of your child's life he will be full of self-doubt and will be trying to find his way, so if you can find a positive slant on things, he will always respond better to that than if you are always critical of him. But it can be very difficult to do this at times. Make sure you are sincere about what you say, as children are quite perceptive and can very easily see through their parents if you aren't. There will of course be many periods of anxiety and doubt as a teenager, so your positive and constructive comments will help keep his confidence levels as high as possible.

Life Jacket

You should try to empathise with his lifestyle and the things he enjoys doing as much as possible. Be careful not to condemn and be disrespectful to his personal tastes because you don't happen to like them yourself.

Social media, trust and your Teenager

It is very important to keep track of what your teenage children are doing, the dangers and pitfalls are everywhere. Your instinct is to protect them, but how can you do this and know what's going on, yet still keep their trust in you? It is a huge dilemma, and managed badly can be potentially disastrous. When they first want to register to be on Facebook, I suggest you make it a condition that they accept you as a 'friend'. You can explain that this is so you can keep track of where they are and what they get up to. They will not be happy with this at first, but if you don't abuse this situation, they will eventually accept it.

Explain that you will not be following their every activity, it is only because you care about and love them so much. Tell them that you trust them to use the internet wisely, and that you are confident that they will not abuse it. By giving them autonomy and responsibility over how they use social media sites it will encourage them to respect the boundaries and not abuse your trust in them.

You can be very discreet while following them and their friends on whichever social media sites they are on and keep yourself well under the radar. You should try to avoid communicating directly with them via any of the forms of social media, to avoid getting involved in their social life. But this can still be a very useful tool to observe and be aware of what they and their friends get up to at parties and when they are out socialising.

If you are informed like this, it can help you advise (but never order) your children with whom they should spend their time. This becomes a lot more difficult as they get older, but if your relationship is really strong, and if you have really worked at it as they have grown up, then you can still influence them, through these years and into their adulthood.

In my opinion, this is one of the most important pieces of advice I can offer you during the whole of your child's upbringing, and potentially it can save a terrible situation from developing. The computer that your child uses should never be hidden away in the corner of a room, and certainly never in their bedroom, at least until they are much older, 16+. It could be placed in the kitchen, or another room where there are always family members moving around in it. This way you can always see what websites they are looking at, and with whom they are communicating online. It will also help stop them spending too much time in their bedrooms and doing things on the quiet. It will allow you to retain a degree of control over them and the internet. 'Knowledge is everything', and the more you know what your children do online, the safer and better it will be for everyone. It may not even be your children who are behaving in a silly manner, but other people with ulterior motives, encouraging them to behave irresponsibly.

Even with having this control measure in place, it is not certain that you can monitor 100% who they are in contact with online. We always had this guideline in place in our house, and despite this, my daughter managed to make friends with a man online, who was pretending to be her age, 14. He was trying to convince her to get on a train and go to Manchester to meet him. We lived in Surrey at the time. Fortunately, by luck, while I was walking behind her in the kitchen, and she was at the screen, I was able to read part of a conversation thread on Facebook. We just managed to avoid a potentially very dangerous episode with our daughter. We were very lucky! But if she had been alone in her bedroom online, who knows what might have happened.

Life Jacket

You should only ever have the computer your children use in the kitchen, or another very well used room in your home.

Another strategy which worked very well for me and my children was that up to the age of 16 we did not to allow them to keep their mobile phones in their bedrooms after their official bedtimes. This was introduced the day they got their first mobiles, and because they were so pleased at finally getting a mobile phone, it was never questioned until they were much older, 16+. The phone can easily be recharged overnight in the kitchen or another room in the house and then in the morning they would get it back.

This will stop your child texting his friends, or worse still, people he doesn't know but is in contact with through social media, when you are not around and he should be sleeping. Of course, he can still do this during the day, but at least it will not disturb his night. It will allow him to have that undisturbed night's sleep, and ensure he is fresh for school the next day. Remember, your teenager needs plenty of sleep as his body is developing rapidly during this period of his life, and growing up can be a very tiring business.

Up to the age of 16, if you can, it is worthwhile trying to avoid any TV's in your child's bedroom as well. This was another rule that we introduced very early on in their childhood. I did this, as when I got home from work and not having seen them all day, I wanted to play and chat with my children, and not have them 'hidden away' elsewhere in the house so they didn't know I was home. I admit that this was motivated by selfishness, but it always relaxed me seeing and playing with my children when I got home from work. So this worked for our family, as we introduced it at a very young age and because of this it was never questioned as it was the household norm. Although often they would say to us that their friends had a TV in their rooms. I would always reply that families are different and you have things that your friends do not have. They understood this and that everybody is not necessarily the same. They also reluctantly accepted this rule.

If you are to try and introduce these household rules you need to do it at a very early age, before they become teenagers. So try to control what they are looking at on screen and on the internet when they first start using a computer. If it is introduced early on in their childhood it will become one of the standard non-negotiable rules of the house, and will never be questioned. Even if they do not like it and 'all their friends have one', they will accept it.

The Minefield of Boyfriends and Girlfriends

Once Boyfriends or Girlfriends become a part of your child's life, the subject of when to have sex has to be discussed. Initially, this will be very embarrassing for both of you, but you mustn't avoid talking about it. Start with an open ended question in a relaxed environment at the dinner table. Ask a question such as 'when do you think the right time to start having sex is?' Follow it up with a question starting with 'Why?' After your child has said what he thinks, you can then offer your opinion, but make sure you emphasise how much you respect your child's point of view.

If your child says "I'm not discussing this with you now", suggest another time when you both agree that you will talk about it. But don't just let it go after that.

Lifebuoy

It is very important that you do not let the subject of when to have sex get forgotten about, as your child needs to be fully aware of the risks, and what responsible behaviour involves. This is equally as important for your daughter as it is for your son.

It is very important that you accept your child's choice of Boyfriend or Girlfriend, however much your gut instinct says the opposite. If your child has made her choice, you have to respect her decision. You can express your concerns to her, but never try to force your opinions on her. In any case it will backfire on you and she will do what she wants.

If your daughter has got to the stage of going out with a boy, and she is happy with the situation, then you must respect the fact that they are together, however difficult that is for you. If you are open and tolerant with her, she will respect the boundaries that you have set together. If you are hostile right from the beginning, she is far more likely not to listen to your advice and do something silly.

I made the mistake of trying to prevent my daughter going out with a boy who was three years older than her, when she was only 15. It was for all the right reasons, or so I thought. I was very vociferous about it, and made sure both of them knew I didn't approve of him. All I did was alienate her for a few months, as she stopped talking to me about anything significant. It was like purgatory to watch her going out with this boy, and know that I had no influence on the situation. Not a nice feeling for a father at all.

Eventually when she broke up with him, I apologised to her and admitted my mistake. Fortunately, after a few weeks, things got back to normal with her, and she started talking openly to me again.

It was very poor Fatherhood on my part, and I learnt a lot from it. And even though I've never made the same mistake again, when she's annoyed with me, she still reminds me of this.

Keeping the Lines of Communication open at all times.

Teenage children are a real challenge for fathers (and mothers), as sometimes, actually very often, they can be quite irrational and unmanageable. It is now that all the work and skills you have learned and put in over the years can pay dividends. Keep communicating with your child and never take the easy option of just closing off the dialogue and 'farming' them out to others. Or worse still, sending them away to be looked after by other people, because you can't be bothered to resolve the issues.

Although your child will sometimes 'Hate you', she doesn't really, despite this she still really needs your guidance. If you end up having an argument with her, don't keep forcing your point of view on her. Once you have said your piece, stop going on about it and give yourself and your child space to cool off. You can always resort to the Drinks Coaster if it is really getting out of hand and neither of you will back down. Very often however, after things have calmed down, it will result in you or your child saying sorry, whichever one of you is in the wrong. Remember with your child, there is no need to be proud when you are in the wrong, so if you are, just admit it.

Once the emotion of a particular situation has subsided and you have both had a chance to reflect on what it was about, it never seems so serious. Each time this happens, it will just serve to strengthen your bonds with your child, and if it is with your daughter, she will respect you even more as her father, even if she doesn't want to admit it.

Life Raft

You must face up to issues, and not put them off UNTIL another day, hoping that they will go away. Good open communication will always save the day.

Remember, during the teenage years the dynamic between you and your daughter will be very combustible, as you know how vulnerable she is, while very often she cannot see it at all. This is very much the case around boys, particularly as you know exactly what they are thinking about her, because you were once that age and had the same thoughts about girls. Tolerance and respect between you both is key to your relationship during these years.

When my daughter was 15, she went out with her first boyfriend on a date to the local cinema. I said to her that she must text me to say when the film had finished and I would come and pick them both up. She got so wrapped up in the date, that she didn't text me as agreed. I was very worried, so I jumped in my car and drove to the cinema and subsequently caught up with her and her boyfriend who were walking back home.

I reacted instinctively and without thinking, put my headlights on full beam and drove slowly behind them both for about 15 minutes, at walking pace, all the way home. This was extremely embarrassing for them both, as well as myself. But it got the message over to her. She was furious with me for several days afterwards, and didn't talk to me. But from then onwards, she has always texted me to tell me where she is and at the agreed time when she is supposed to.

This is quite a high risk strategy though, because she could have reacted very badly and closed up to me for much longer than a few days. This would have been very challenging for me, so depending on the situation, you need to weigh the potential benefits up against the potential risks, and then follow your instinct.

Life Jacket

Make sure your child knows the ground rules for certain situations, and if they are not respected, then you must take the appropriate action.

Teenagers experiment with stuff!

During the teenage years, it is normal that your child will want to try new things and experiment. This is part of growing up. But you must keep encouraging your child to always talk to you when he wants to try things, whether it is smoking, sex, alcohol or drugs. It is very important that you get him to talk before he tries it, as opposed to afterwards. If you have developed a strong open relationship with your child because you have been so closely involved during his younger years, then he should be happy to talk to you about these things, even though it may still be a little uncomfortable. He will very probably do them anyway, depending on his peer group of friends, so if possible, encourage him to try them in a controlled environment at home. However, avoid him trying drugs anywhere if you possibly can, as there will be less risk.

Sit down with your child and oversee him having his first drink, or cigarette. Use it as a learning experience together, where you can discuss the effects and consequences of smoking or drinking. If it is your child's first sexual experience, encourage him to do it in the safety and privacy of his bedroom at home, rather than elsewhere in a potentially public, embarrassing or dangerous place.

This is particularly important if you have a daughter, although of course it is also for your son. Sometimes, the reality will not match the perception of how her first sexual experience should be. Therefore, she will need emotional support from you and her mother, which is best done in the privacy and intimacy of your own home.

Lifebuoy

By encouraging your child to have her first sexual experience at home, you and your partner can be there, IF needed, to give her emotional support afterwards.

It could happen that you find out that your child is already drinking with his friends and just hasn't told you, because he knows what you will say. If this is happening you must address the matter as soon as possible. You will need to choose your moment and sit down with him and find out exactly why he is doing this, particularly as it's 'on the quiet'. The answer may well be because of peer pressure. He is doing it because all his friends are and he doesn't want to be the odd one out, which could lead to him potentially being ostracised by his group of friends. Peer pressure with teenagers is not to be underestimated.

Once you have sat down with him, he needs to understand about the effects of alcohol on him, particularly as he is not used to it. You will need to explain to him that it can be harmful and why he must start to drink responsibly. Encourage him to stand up and not to be afraid to say "no" to a drink from time to time. Initially, his friends may tease him a bit, but if they are real friends, then they will probably respect him even more, as he will be seen as being 'his own man'.

Becoming withdrawn or depressed can very easily occur during your child's teenage years and can be a sign that something isn't right. If your child is used to spending most of his hours at home in his room, this may be quite difficult to spot. So if this

happens, it may be down to strained relationships with his friends at school, or a negative sense of self perception, due to such things as being slightly overweight, having acne or greasy hair. It could be the smallest of things that triggers this, or it could be something more serious.

If you miss the initial signs with your child it may be years before you are able to rectify the situation. It will of course help immensely if you are still making sure you all eat evening meals together, because this time remains a vital opportunity to observe and learn about each other's day. Still kissing your child goodnight will also help you to identify if something doesn't seem quite right. Any behavioural changes will be easily identified if you are regularly together at the dinner table. If you still keep doing the 'Best and Worst' game as well, you will continue to be learning about what is going on in your teenagers' life.

Being depressed, uncommunicative or secretive may also be a warning sign for excessive drinking or even drug use. If your child becomes withdrawn and is not his normal self, you will need to act quite quickly to avoid the situation spiralling out of control. This is where your skills as a Father will be really tested. You cannot shy away from confronting the issue, so you must try to bring it out into the open as quickly as possible. The first thing to do is try to talk about it with your child, but in a relaxed situation. Forcing a conversation however, that your child does not want to have, could result in completely the opposite effect to the one you want to achieve.

Life Jacket

It is very important to be observant. You must always be on the look-out for changes in your child's behaviour.

Dinner time is always a good moment to raise difficult issues, as everyone is seated at the table, and usually fairly relaxed. If this doesn't work, then try in the morning just after your child has woken up. He will be far more receptive at this time of day after a good night's sleep. Find out the reasons why he is drinking or taking drugs by asking open ended questions, and try to decide together how it can be handled. Examples of these questions can be found in the Appendix.

You may, however, need to seek Professional help depending on your assessment of the situation. But once identified, the situation can be addressed immediately, and you can then decide what course of action needs to be taken.

Sharing fun times with your Teenager

Once a year, every year, sharing something very special and enjoyable with your child will reinforce your closeness together. Doing this individually and separately for each of your children will make it more meaningful to them. Try to do something they really like doing. For example, you could go away for the day to the beach and see the amusements and shows, or into London shopping for the day. Even if you hate shopping, make the effort for your child.

This will reinforce the bond you have with your child and continue to bring you even closer together. This is uninterrupted quality time for you both and will be enjoyed and valued by the two of you for many years. In fact, there is no time or age limit on this. It can even be done when your child has moved out and has her own family. It is a time when you can both enjoy each other's company without any of the pressures of home or school life. It will also be a time when you will be able to discuss any subjects which you feel like. Your child is very likely to open up with you on some areas you don't usually talk about, because she feels so relaxed and there is no pressure. Of course, you can also do the same.

Chapter 7

<u>Help Me – She's leaving home</u>

This is a very challenging time in your child's development, as he can hardly wait to be independent. Yet he still needs you financially and emotionally. He believes that he is ready for the outside world and therefore you should be feeling very proud of what you have achieved together. You have given that belief to him through the love and care that you have surrounded him with while he has been growing up. So it is now the time he needs to feel that you are not holding him back, but encouraging and supporting him as he faces the different type of challenges that lay ahead of him.

<u>Your child is legally an adult</u>

It is true that occasionally you will both have some very direct and even unpalatable things to say to each other. Don't worry, this is completely normal if you have fostered a strong and open communication philosophy with your child. So it is very important that you keep an open dialogue with him and that the quality of the communication that you have built together is never closed off. This will cause a lot of friction between you at times, particularly as he has an unflinching desire to be treated like an adult. He believes that he is an adult, which of course he is, even though he lacks the experience and sometimes doesn't behave like an adult.

But you know that although he is legally an adult, he still has a lot to learn about life and it is your responsibility to continue to guide him and help him learn this, while never putting him down. At this stage, your role as a father is developing very much into an advisory one and you need to be on hand to offer him advice (not a lecture), on any subject. These can be on subjects as diverse as Work, University, Relationships, (both long term and short), Housing, Friendships, Money, etc., and the list goes on. How you handle this stage of his development will influence strongly how his relationship with you and his mother develops over the next few years.

It is not an easy time for him, as he might be living away from home, or maybe at University or in a rented place having just started work. He is finding his way in life, independent from you and his mother, and although on the outside he may appear very confident of himself, on the inside he may be full of doubts. So when he comes home, having been away, remember he will have got used to doing what he wants, when he wants and not being told what to do. So this is a very delicate balancing act that you will have to manage.

It is important, however, that when he is home, he still contributes to the household chores, even though he can't be bothered to do them when you need them done. He may be impatient when you ask him to do things, so the important thing is not to turn this necessity to contribute into a confrontation, in order to get things done. The secret is to approach him when he is relaxed, possibly at dinner time and calmly explain the need for him to help out while he is at home. Try to avoid raising your voice to him, as this will only raise the chance of one of you losing your cool. Once you have explained what you expect him to do, don't go on about it. He will have heard what you said and only if he doesn't do what is expected, should you need to discuss it with him again.

Life Jacket

Keep an open dialogue with your child and ensure that the quality of your communication together does not diminish through confrontation. Keep cool and calm at all times.

Your child wants to be Independent, and is probably ready to be, but for young people today, it is a real challenge to actually make that transition. Therefore, it is vital that you are there at all times to help him become the master of his own destiny.

Empathise, sympathise, but don't criticise

Part of growing up is going out on your own and discovering new things in the world. New adventures and new people are all part of it. Encourage her to do this at every opportunity. Don't try to keep her cooped up at home and prevent her from experiencing these new things, as she will only become resentful about it. Usually, this starts after A-levels, or after University. Travelling is a good way for her to do this. If she does this after she has finished her degree, when she is bit more mature, she may get more out of it and it is a good time just before she starts her first job.

She will be curious to know what it is like to go away and discover things on her own, although at the same time she will be apprehensive. She may show it, or sometimes she may try to hide it. So it is your job to reassure her that she should go ahead and try these new experiences, however difficult it will feel for you to be encouraging her to do this.

She doesn't have to go to the other side of the world, as each child is different. It might just be to a neighbouring country for a couple of weeks, but the important thing is that she is doing it by herself, or maybe with a good friend. It doesn't have to be expensive to travel, but at this age it will be an invaluable part of her growing up process and her transition to independence. It will give her the confidence to meet new challenges and experience new things, and will definitely contribute to the transition from childhood to adulthood.

Life Jacket

Encourage your child to spread her wings and broaden her horizons, by travelling and experiencing new cultures and places.

It is natural to want to be over-protective to your child, but you must let him go, so he can experience both the rough and the smooth side of life. Resist the urge to be too curious and appear to be hassling him to tell you what he is doing. He will be happy to tell you if you have done the groundwork in his formative years.

Explain to him that you are interested in what he is doing, as opposed to wanting to try to control him. But make sure you back up these words with actions, and don't end up doing the opposite. Even though he is older now he still needs to know that you will always be there to help him out if he gets into a tricky situation. He will seek your advice out when he feels he needs it and you should always try to be available to give it. But he will go his own way eventually and it should be with your blessing.

Part of branching out on your own is making mistakes. You did this, and your child will too, and he will learn from them just like you did. Whatever mistakes he makes, and however disappointed it makes you feel, resist the urge to criticise him. Just be available to help him sort it out. For example, he might have gone out drinking with his friends the night before and missed his train to work the next day and been late for that important business meeting.

When he does do this, or something else, which is inevitable at his age, be ready to help him rectify his mistake. It may mean you have to drive him to the station in your dressing gown early in the morning to catch the later train. Or you might suggest things that he can say to his boss to explain what has happened and help him limit the damage. Encourage him to be honest and say that you are sure his boss will give him another chance. He will know whether his boss is really like that, but we have all made mistakes, including his boss.

If he knows he can always rely on you to be there if things go wrong, he will be encouraged to become his own man and make his own way in the world. He will always be secure in the knowledge that if things don't go to plan, you, his father, are there as the safety net.

Your child is your equal

Remember that your child is now an adult and she will be very observant of what is going on around her. Maintaining the philosophy of being totally open in communication with your child, irrespective of the subject matter in discussion, will help the changing family dynamic. No subject must ever be 'off the table'. Don't hide things from her, she will know what is going on. So whatever the situation, be open and honest. She will really value this going forward.

You might be having problems in your own relationship, and if so, be open. Explain to her, preferably together with your partner, exactly what is going on, and what you are both doing to try and rectify it. It is much better for her if she understands the situation and is not guessing what is going on, even if she doesn't particularly like what she is hearing.

As you get older and technology evolves, your child will certainly have expertise in areas that you don't. You should encourage him to teach you things and share his knowledge with you in areas that you are not fully confident or informed about. For example, it could be setting up a blog or website, or even fixing a car engine. He will really value this approach from you and will feel that you really do treat him as an adult and an equal.

It will strengthen the relationship you have with him immeasurably, as the dynamic between you continues to evolve.

Life Jacket

The more your child feels you consider her your equal, the more she will actually become your equal.

A question from you to your daughter like, "What do you think I should do in this instance?" will reinforce her sense of responsibility and she will feel a real sense of pride and satisfaction that you are actually interested in what she thinks. Start asking your child for her advice, she will love this and it will make her feel much closer to you. It will also make her understand that you respect her opinion and that you really are 'treating her like an adult'. The more she feels she is your equal, the more she actually will be. This is very important as she goes out into the world on her own.

Create quality time with your adult child

With so much going on in your child's life, it is really important to create high quality moments for you both to share together. For example, make the effort to do something really special with him once or twice a year. If you have more than one child, make sure you do this with each one of them, but separately. By doing this regularly, each one will feel it is a special time just for them and you to be together.

You should choose activities which you and your child really enjoy doing. For example, these could be things like fishing, going shopping, playing golf, or visiting places together. This will be quality time together when you are both very relaxed, and you will find that conversation on any subject flows very easily.

Lifebuoy

Make the effort to do something special together with your child at least once a year.

Even though your child is now a semi-independent adult, it is still very important to keep telling her that you love her. Whatever is happening in her life, knowing that she is loved will be a huge source of strength to her. You remain a very important part of her life and are the bridge between her childhood and her adulthood. She will still love to hear you say "I love you" and it will continue to be a point of reassurance as her own role in life evolves. You can never say "I love you" too often to your son or daughter, whatever age they are.

When your child comes home to see you, try to maintain as many of the little routines you did when he was a child. For example, small things like kissing him good night and good morning, or playing a game on his console with him. These will ensure that he knows that whatever life throws at him, there are very solid points of reference at home and he will always be secure in that environment. If your child has his own room or shares a room with a sibling, make sure that his room continues to be 'his', with his things still in it. This will be a refuge for him in the future when he needs it, as he comes across the inevitable challenges that life will throw at him. It will remain a place for him to be able to go which is familiar, welcoming and secure.

Life Raft

Whatever is happening in your child's life, make sure you continue to use those reassuring words 'I love you'.

She's an adult now

Your child will be very pleased to have someone who is always a consistent part of her life. So try not to change the habits of a lifetime, at least the good ones. Try to get rid of the bad ones however. For example, when she comes home, continue to make sure you all eat the evening meal together. This will remain a huge source of information for you in adulthood, like it has always been while she was growing up. She will open up about what is going on in her life, as well as you being able to tell her what is happening in yours. This interaction will never become redundant and will ensure a certain continuity in terms of open communication with your child.

This has always been important while your child has been growing up, but it is even more so now, as the stakes are so much higher for him. As an adult, if he makes a serious error, it could result in him losing a job, or ruining a relationship with a partner or business contact. Listening and being open is doubly important now. Your child still needs to know that he can turn to you when things don't go quite to plan. Knowing you will listen, evaluate the situation with him and offer some practical advice based on your many years of experience will reassure him hugely.

Life Jacket

One of the most important skills you can practice now your child is an adult, is the art of listening.

Chapter 8

Help - My Children Have Grown Up

You are still a Father

The house will suddenly feel empty once they finally take all their belongings and leave home, but this doesn't mean that your role as a father has come to the end. You will still see them regularly, but just in a different light, in different circumstances and in different places. If you have nurtured the strong bonds with your child as he has grown up, he will want to keep seeing you and will make the effort to facilitate you seeing him. Of course, you wouldn't have got this far with this book if that wasn't one of your goals as a father.

As the dynamic is so different now to when he was a child and living at home, doing things together becomes an even more important part of your ongoing relationship. You can enjoy a meal or a drink out together in a relaxed atmosphere, which will allow you to chat about what is going on in each other's lives and will help you remain relevant to each other. As your adult child's life gets busier and busier, opportunities for you and him to discuss things that really matter become less numerous. So even though your own life may be very busy, continue to try to make yourself available to spend time with him.

Life Jacket

Doing things together will help keep you close to your child even though he has now left home.

He still needs to know that you are always around for him, even if he doesn't actually say it, so don't forget to tell him that. You can become a huge source of information, reference and even inspiration for your child. If you have built up a strong and mutually respectful relationship with him throughout his childhood, these years can be very satisfying for both of you as you adapt to each others changing circumstances. Remember though, that your child is an independent adult now, so be careful not to try to impose your ideas on him. Simply be there to prompt and provoke thought.

<u>**Why change a habit of a lifetime?**</u>

When your child was a little boy, you were always available for him during the Festive period, so why change a habit of a lifetime? He and his family can now come to you, or you go to theirs, but make sure you always make the effort at this time of year. Continue to try to keep Christmas and New Year special for the whole family. It really is that 'once a year' time for families of all generations to be together.

Even though your children are now adults, try to ensure that at least once a year, you all go on holiday together, or a short break as a family. Depending on what budget you have available, it could be anywhere. The important thing is not the location, but the fact that you are all together in a relaxed environment. This will keep you close, and allow you to spend quality time together outside of your respective normal home environments. Everyone will be in a holiday mood, so it should result in very high quality time that you spend together.

Life Jacket

Keep Christmas a special time for all the family whatever age they are.

If you have always done this, and it has always been enjoyed by everyone, your children, their partners and family will be very happy to join you. Of course, if you are paying for the holiday that will be even better for them.

<u>**You are your child's Lifebuoy**</u>

First and foremost, always be available for your child when she needs you. Now she is totally independent and running her own life she will only need you when it is really important to her, and she is perhaps struggling to manage. Always being there will reassure her that she is not alone when she comes across a situation that she hasn't encountered before. It is important that you continue to encourage her, help her and offer her potential solutions to the issues she is facing. These could be as diverse as illness, financial worries, relationship problems or even issues with her own children.

When she has her own family, and in particular children, remember how it was for you when you first had yours. She will need help and advice on how to manage many very basic day to day things. By always being there for her, it will allow you to establish some new bonds for yourself, namely, being a Grandfather. This is a wonderful relationship to nurture and develop with your grandchildren and has a completely different dynamic to the one when you first became a father. You literally can have all the fun with none of the responsibilities. Once they become a bit too hard work, and you are getting tired, you can simply hand them back. Actually, it's not exactly like that, but it's not far off.

Lifebuoy

Always be there for your child. She still needs you even though she is now an adult.

If it makes your child happy, then you should be happy

Encourage your child in whatever career he wants to do. If it makes him happy, then you must support him, even if you don't necessarily agree with his choice. Let him establish himself and try not to be always on top of him asking him how it is going. Even though he is much older now, it is still always a good strategy to ask open ended general questions about his career. This will encourage him to start up a discussion, or prompt thought on the issue. But try not to force your opinions on him. This will backfire spectacularly if you do, because even though he is an Independent adult, inside him he will not like feeling as if he is being treated like a child again, even if that is not your intention at all.

Always make a big effort to get on with your child's partner. If she has chosen somebody, it is because she believes he is the right person for her and brings her happiness. Even if you have a bad gut feeling, or simply don't like him (it happens sometimes that we just don't get on with some people), you must never make your feelings known, and must just 'bite your tongue' and make the effort for your child.

It can be absolutely soul destroying if you find that when your child is an adult, you never see her because you don't get on with her partner. So if for no other reason apart from the fact you love your daughter unreservedly, try to make the effort to 'like' him. It will certainly not be easy sometimes, but remember, if your daughter has chosen him, then you have to respect her choice and get on with him. The alternative if you don't, is that you may see your daughter much less, or worse still, never at all.

Learn from your mistakes

You have something that your child does not yet possess and that has taken you many years to acquire, namely wisdom and experience. Just because he is adult it doesn't mean that you are no longer very relevant to your child's life. In fact, at times, you are even more than you or your child actually realise. Your presence, by just being around, can be an inspiration as well as a security valve for him.

You will have made mistakes along the way, both with your children, and in your life generally. There is a strong chance that you will have come across most situations in some guise or another. Therefore, it is when your child encounters one of these, that you can really make a meaningful contribution to his life situation.

It might be the death of a grandparent who was very close to your child and a big emotional support for him. You will be able to offer advice on how to handle the emotion and grief, particularly if it is the first time that your child has experienced such an event. You will be able to explain that coping with the death of a loved one is part of life generally, however emotionally hard it is to handle. You can help your child manage, and prepare him to be able to cope with this kind of situation when it occurs again.

It could be the break-up of his marriage or a long term relationship. Emotionally, these situations can be very difficult to manage, but the fact that you are there and can offer some advice will make the pain easier to bear. At times like this, listening is the most important skill you have. Just letting him talk, however long it takes and whatever he actually says, will help him start to come to terms with the situation he is facing. Be careful not to force your advice on your child however, but make sure he knows you are there to help whenever he needs you. You will know when your child is in pain, as you will sense it as well. In these situations, you really feel the anguish of your child, and it hurts you as well, because you can actually feel quite helpless at times.

A little while ago, I was discussing one of my children with a good friend of mine, as he had just broken up with his long term partner and was taking it very badly. I was very concerned for my son, as I could feel his pain so acutely. My friend said to me something which really summed up exactly how I felt. "You know, Mark, if you have children, they will all have ups and downs and ultimately you are only as happy as your unhappiest child". He was so right. Not only from a father's perspective, but a parents generally. Whatever the age of your child, this sentiment is true throughout their entire life.

Life Jacket

Simply listening and being there for your child will help him overcome some very difficult situations whatever his age.

Afterword

<u>Help Me – My job is done, or is it?</u>

Every child wants to have a great relationship with their father, but sometimes this doesn't always work out. The goal of this book therefore has been to offer some advice and tips which, whatever your life achievements are, can help you to increase the quality of your life with your children. Irrespective of what age they are, a high quality father/child relationship leads to the ultimate fulfilment as a person.

This book started as an idea which came about because my father travelled a lot when I was a child. Things were different in those days. Despite that, I missed the interaction with him, the sharing of my achievements and all those special intimate moments that only a father can share with his child. So I was determined to ensure that I would be there for all those key moments with my children; if I was lucky enough to have any. So this book has been a culmination of my desire to give my children what I felt I lacked during my own childhood, and my desire to pass on my experiences for the benefit of other fathers.

It has been an opportunity to share anecdotes and discuss tactics and strategies for dealing with those challenging moments. Whether your child is in the 'terrible two's', a complex teenager, or an adult who has started his own life away from home. Problems which in the moment can seem insurmountable can be overcome. Hopefully, I have achieved this goal.

With your children, you are judged and determined by the little things you do with them. Details matter. It is not the size of the home you live in, or the salary you earn or the value of the Christmas presents you give them. It is the time you give them, the respect that you treat them with and above all, the love and security you offer them as they grow up and pass through the daily challenges of childhood. It is the example you set them as they observe you while they grow up. The expression 'Your children are what you make them', both consciously and unconsciously, is so true, and we as parents must never forget that.

The most precious gift you can give a child as a father (parent), is time and it costs you nothing at all. How often do children reach adulthood and the father looks back and says "it went so fast, and I missed so much"? Make

sure you don't let that happen with your child. The very fact you have got
to the end of this book, shows that you have no intention of letting this
happen with you.

Lifebuoy

The most precious gift that you can give to your child while he grows up is
your time.

So please go out there and talk to other fathers and encourage them and
spread the word to get involved in every aspect of their children's lives.
Remember, each child needs a dad just as much as he needs his mum. By
doing this with your own children, you will enrich their lives
immeasurably and help them become successful adults in their own right.
You will also enrich your own existence. You will have prepared your
child to go out in life, take charge of his own destiny and contribute fully
to society as a well-balanced and considerate individual.

Appendix

<u>**Hearn's Agreement**</u>

<u>Date here</u>

We agree to do the following every day:

- Tidy room completely before going to bed.

- Make bed every morning.

- Feed dogs & do dishwasher duty when it's my turn without being reminded by mummy and daddy.

- Hang any school clothes up immediately from getting home from school.

- No leaving of school bags, tennis bags, shoes in the hall.

- No rudeness, swearing or aggression towards mummy and daddy or each other.

- No wrappers/yoghurt pots/food etc. to be left in bedrooms and playroom.

- All homework to be done before any TV is watched.

- Every shower time must hang towels up afterwards and clothes (dirty or clean) sorted and put away.

- When mummy and daddy ask for help, we do so from time to time, and not always say "no".

- Share laying and clearing the table at every meal time.

- Prepare all school bags the night before.

Punishment if we do not do all of the above tasks:

- Grounded for one week.

- Half an hour to bed early.

- No TV for between a day and a week.

- Confiscation of mobile phone for between 1 and 7 days.

We accept the contents of this contract, and will not argue with any punishment given.

Signed

Christophe Hearn - Clarissa Hearn - Guillaume Hearn

Daddy - Mummy

P.S If we comply with all of our tasks during one week, mummy and daddy agree to give the PlayStation back for one hour on Saturday and one hour on Sunday for Christophe and Guillaume and for Clarissa to go out with mummy and daddy to somewhere of her choice.

Additional Game Ideas to Amuse Toddlers in the Car

Here are some ideas for family games that you can play in the car when your Toddler/Young Child is bored or misbehaving, and you have exhausted all other options. Your children will love them:

- Learning the alphabet, and reciting it out loud

- Learning the alphabet backwards and reciting it out loud

- Choosing a letter, then saying a wild animal that starts with it. The next person then says an animal with the last letter of the animal chosen by the person before. Depending on your child's age, this could be countries, cars, flowers, colours, or anything else you might choose

- Writing one word on a piece of paper and then folding it and passing it to the next person to do the same. After everyone has done this four times, someone reads out the sentence formed. It will be hilarious. The driver is not included in this game of course!

- Calling out basic maths questions (depending on the age of your child) but they can be varying levels of difficulty e.g 3 + 8? Or 54 - 26? Or 7 x 9? This can go on for as long as you need it to.

- Car snooker. Looking for the colours of cars, based on the order the coloured balls are played in snooker

- Looking for certain makes of car on the road, chosen by Dad of course!

- Singing songs that have to start exactly and finish between two defined points on the road, for example 'ten little ducks went swimming one day' through the Dartford or Mersey Tunnel starting when you enter the tunnel and finishing exactly as you come out of it

- Naming different types of Dinosaurs. The difficulty can depend on the age of your children

- Naming farm animals and the places where they live on the farm

- Naming Capital cities around the world, or calling out the city and asking which country

A Few Ideas of Story Themes to tell your children in the car when they are bored

- The 'Wicked Witch of Gott' – if you pull a face as you go to school, she casts a spell on you and you can't change your face until you apologise to her personally. So you end up going to school with a strange face, get into trouble with the teachers for pulling faces all day. How you say sorry. Learning to be polite, and learning from your experience.

- An adventure of a Dinosaur family through pre-historic times, travelling from Nirvana to Utopia. They come across challenges such as being attacked by Tyrannosaurus Rex's or Velociraptors. Hide and seek to evade them. Brontosaurus beats them by slapping his neck and knocking them over. Travelling through mountainous terrain, then prairie lands etc.

- A family of racing cars travelling across Europe together to get to an important race in Monaco. Their adventures to get there. Flat tyres, broken windscreens, no petrol, oil leak, break downs. How you overcome these to get to race on time. Each member of the family is a different car.

- A family of little people travelling through a land of Giants, and their efforts to overcome huge obstacles and avoid being trodden upon. This is inspired by the book Gulliver's Travels, but you can invent any adventures for the family to go through.

- A family of dogs whose owners move away and forget them all at the old house. Their travels and adventures to finally be reunited with their owners. Just their sense of love and loyalty eventually guides them to their new home. You can invent many adventures, both dangerous and fun as they find their way. This is inspired by the book The Incredible Journey.

Open ended Questions to ask when your teenager is struggling to manage her life

How is it going with your friends at school?

What kinds of things do you do when you are at their place?

What do you do when you go out with your friends?

What do you think about drug taking and young people?

What do you think the appeal of drugs is to young people?

Why do you want to try drugs?

Where do you go to use your drugs?

How does it feel when you are using drugs?

Why do you feel the need to get drunk?

How many of your friends smoke?

Who do you sit with at lunchtime when you are at school?

How do you get on with your teachers at school?

Who is your favourite teacher at school?

Who is your worst teacher at school and why?

How is it going with your boyfriend/girlfriend?

Acknowledgements

The only place to start for a book like this is with my three children, Christophe, Clarissa and Guillaume. Thank you for inspiring me to write this book on fatherhood. Together you have given me so much joy (and heartache) on this journey through life with you, as you have grown up under my eyes. It was amazing and enriching and it is still set to go on for many years to come.

I also have to give special thanks to Clarissa for starting the process of typing the initial manuscript and launching the long process which has resulted in this book finally being published.

Then I have to thank my wife Corinne, who has been so patient with me while I have spent the thousands of hours writing this book. She has provided me with many cups of tea to keep me going on numerous occasions, when my motivation has been waning. This is not to mention her partnership with me on this incredible voyage we have taken together as parents to our children. This book is a culmination of that journey.

I also need to thank my many friends for supporting this venture and listening to me incessantly while I used them as sounding boards for my ideas. Not one of you has ever tried to discourage me to give up the dream of this project.

Finally, an immense debt of gratitude to my friend Michael Heppell, who guided me through the whole process from idea to realisation and without whose input the finished article would have been very different. Thank you, Michael.

If you have any feedback on my book or the subject matter, please contact me through my Blog helpimafather.wordpress.com.

Thank you

Mark Hearn